ESSENTIAL
LONDON

 Best places to see 34–55

 Featured sight

 St James's, Mayfair and Piccadilly 75–92

 Knightsbridge, Kensington and Chelsea 127–140

 The City and East 93–110

 Covent Garden, Bloomsbury and Soho 141–156

 Westminster and the South Bank 111–126

Outer London 157–171

Original text by Paul Murphy

Revised and updated by Paul Wade and Kathy Arnold

© AA Media Limited 2010
First published 1999. Revised 2010
ISBN 978-0-7495-6522-0

Published by AA Publishing, a trading name of AA Media Limited, whose registered office is Fanum House, Basing View, Basingstoke, Hampshire RG21 4EA. Registered number 06112600.

Colour separation: MRM Graphics Ltd. Printed and bound in Italy by Printer Trento S.r.l.

Find out more about AA Publishing and the wide range of services the AA provides by visiting our website at theAA.com/shop

A04015

Enabled by | Ordnance Survey This product includes mapping data licensed from Ordnance Survey® with the permission of the Controller of Her Majesty's Stationery Office. © Crown copyright 2010. All rights reserved. Licence number 100021153

About this book

Symbols are used to denote the following categories:

✚ map reference to maps on cover

✉ address or location

☎ telephone number

🕒 opening times

💷 admission charge

🍴 restaurant or café on premises or nearby

Ⓜ nearest underground train station

🚌 nearest bus/tram route

🚉 nearest overground train station

⛴ nearest ferry stop

✈ nearest airport

❓ other practical information

ℹ tourist information office

► indicates the page where you will find a fuller description

This book is divided into six sections.

The essence of London pages 6–19
Introduction; Features; Food and drink; Short break including the 10 Essentials

Planning pages 20–33
Before you go; Getting there; Getting around; Being there

Best places to see pages 34–55
The unmissable highlights of any visit to London

Best things to do pages 56–71
Great traditional pubs; Top activities; Places to take the children and more

Exploring pages 72–171
The best places to visit in London, organized by area

Excursions pages 172–183
Places to visit out of town

Maps
All map references are to the maps on the covers. For example, Buckingham Palace has the reference ✚ 9E – indicating the grid square in which it is to be found

Admission prices
Inexpensive (under £5); moderate (£5–£10); expensive (over £10). Museums and galleries listed as free may encourage visitors to leave a donation

Hotel prices
Prices are per room per night: £ budget (under £100); ££ moderate (£100–£200); £££ expensive to luxury (over £200)

Restaurant prices
Prices are for a three-course meal per person without drinks: £ budget (under £25); ££ moderate (£25–£50); £££ expensive (over £50)

Contents

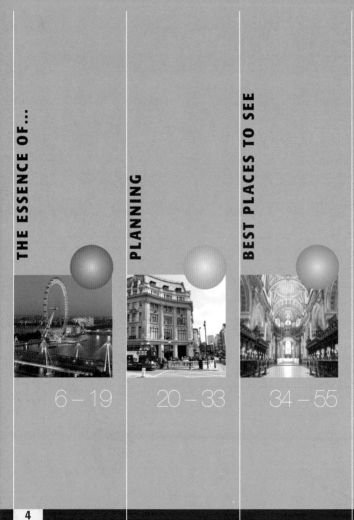

THE ESSENCE OF...

PLANNING

BEST PLACES TO SEE

6 – 19   20 – 33   34 – 55

BEST THINGS TO DO

56 – 71

EXPLORING...

72 – 171

EXCURSIONS

172 – 183

The essence of...

Introduction   8–9

Features   10–11

Food and drink   12–15

Short break   16–19

London is such a varied and cosmopolitan city that there is a bewildering choice of things to do and see. Perhaps inevitably, visitors feel compelled to tick off its major sights at breakneck speed, but this is no way to get the flavour of the city. The key is not to rush, not to feel you have to see it all (you never will) and not to overlook the simple indigenous pleasures of London. Just for a day or two, forget the museums, the historical attractions, and especially the crowded West End stores. Instead, rummage through a street market stall, stroll in the parks and enjoy a pint in a theme-free pub.

features

London mixes ancient and modern with ease, warm, red brick with glass and steel. The great London institutions of the British Museum, the Tower of London, the museums of South Kensington and the Royal Opera House have all undergone major improvements. New landmarks such as the London Eye and the Swiss Re Tower – nicknamed The Gherkin – grace the skyline and London's South Bank and Docklands have sprung to life. Meanwhile, visitors returning to the capital can rest assured that the quiet leafy squares, the parks and the myriad tiny unspoiled churches, pubs and shops soldier timelessly on.

London already boasts world-famous venues, such as Wembley Stadium (association football or soccer), Wimbledon (tennis), Twickenham (rugby union) and Lord's (cricket). Its sports lovers are already looking ahead to 2012, when London hosts the Summer Olympic and Paralympic Games in the East End of the city.

GEOGRAPHY

● London is the largest city in Europe, a ragged oval stretching over 50km (31 miles) across. However, most of 'Visitors' London' is condensed

into Inner London, the area bounded by the underground's Circle Line.

● The best way to see the capital is by a combination of underground (Tube) and walking.

LOCALS AND VISITORS

● London's population reached a peak of around 8.6 million in 1939 then declined slowly to below 7 million in 1983. Only recently has it started to grow again, reaching 7.5 million in 2007 and predicted to rise to 8.9 million by 2031.

● In 2008, London welcomed over 26 million overnight visitors. Nearly 15 million came from overseas for holidays, on business and to study.

● London is a cosmopolitan city, with almost 30 per cent of its population comprising minority ethnic groups.

GOVERNMENT

● Londoners have enjoyed city-wide government since 2000. Political wrangling in the 1980s had led to the previous Greater London Council being abolished by the central government.

● Most local decisions are the responsibility of the 32 borough councils and the City Corporation.

● Croydon is the largest borough with over 350,000 residents. The City of London, covering the square mile in the financial centre, is the smallest with about 8,000.

2012 SUMMER OLYMPICS

● London, hosts in 1908 and 1948, will stage the 2012 Summer Games (27 July–12 August) and the Paralympic Games (29 August–9 September). As well as building five major venues, the Games are a catalyst to redevelop the run-down East End of London and upgrade public transport (www.london2012.com).

food & drink

Long the butt of culinary jokes, the capital's restaurants and British cooking have improved so much in recent years that London is now regarded as among the best places in the world for eating out. The only drawback is that this can be expensive, but fixed-price meals, particularly at lunchtime, can make your pound go very much further.

WHAT TO EAT

The world is your oyster, with representatives from virtually every culinary school on the planet. The most acclaimed generally fall under the banner of Modern European cuisine. When in Britain, however, it would be a shame not to eat British food, from traditional hearty English dishes to the more sophisticated, foreign-influenced, eclectic Modern British cuisine. Long assimilated into mainstream British culture, Indian food should also be on your menu. And of course, at the end of the night look for the local fish and chip shop!

WHERE TO EAT

At the cutting edge of the market the current vogue is for restaurants to boast huge dining rooms, with some likened to ocean liners. Restaurant fashion seems almost as

important as the food itself and a score of London's leading eating houses were created by renowned design guru Sir Terence Conran.

Fashion pervades all the way down the price scale, with yesterday's humble cafés making way for today's trendy cafés. In line with this trend, museum food options have improved enormously in the last few years, too.

If you're on a tight budget, but want to avoid fast food, pop into a pub or grab a picnic of well-prepared salads, sandwiches and more at delis, convenience stores, markets and supermarkets.

WHEN, WHERE AND WHAT TO DRINK

London is no longer straitjacketed by antiquated licensing laws and, consequently, you can drink alcohol at most times of the day or night. As with restaurants, there are any number of different styles of bar, many of the designer variety. Order a cocktail or a soft drink, a bottle of beer or a glass of wine – but watch out for high prices in up-market establishments. London has many fine traditional English pubs serving traditional English beer. At its best, it is hand-drawn from oak casks and is darker, stronger and warmer than lager beers.

BRITISH FOOD

There are places still serving the type of food Charles Dickens would recognize – hot savoury pies, roast meats and game, followed by steamed sweet puddings and pies – though they don't usually come cheap. The traditional British Sunday lunch (roast beef and Yorkshire pudding) is a must; try one of our recommended British restaurants or any good large hotel.

Wherever you are staying you will probably get the chance to start the day the traditional British way, with a cooked breakfast of eggs, bacon and/or sausages, mushrooms, tomatoes and/or baked beans and toast. Afternoon tea is the other great English institution, comprising small thinly sliced sandwiches, scones and/or cake. Nowadays, this ritual is best enjoyed at a glamorous London hotel.

short break

If you only have a short time to visit London and would like to take home some unforgettable memories, you can do something local and capture the real flavour of the city. The following suggestions will give you a wide range of sights and experiences that won't take long, won't cost very much and will make your visit very special.

● **Ride on the top deck of a London bus** – still a great way to see the capital. Ride a No 11 bus between Chelsea, Victoria, Westminster, St Paul's Cathedral and the Bank of England.

● **Cruise on the Thames** – take a river boat ride from Westminster Pier to Greenwich, where the journey is accompanied by a lively commentary.

● **Relax in the park** when the traffic noise grates and your feet begin to ache; escape to Hyde Park, Kensington Gardens, St James's Park or Regent's Park.

● **Join a walking tour** and let a professional guide take you by the hand and lead you through the streets of London. It is the best and most enjoyable way to learn about the capital – and cheap too. Pick up a flyer from a tourist information office or see *Time Out*, a weekly magazine, for details.

● **Visit a traditional London pub**, although it's hard to tell the phonies from the real thing these days (➤ 66 for some suggestions).

● **Take afternoon tea** – the quintessential British afternoon pastime (➤ 61).

● **Attend a church concert**. Even the least God-fearing of folk will find this an uplifting experience.

● **Enjoy the view from Waterloo Bridge** to see St Paul's and the London skyline at their very best.

● **Visit a street market** – two of the best are Brick Lane and Portobello Road, (➤ 61, 110 and 139 for details and more suggestions).

● **Visit the Inns of Court** – not a 'sight' as such, but an astonishing oasis in the heart of the city and a glimpse of 'olde London' that few locals (let alone visitors) ever see (➤ 98 and 100–101).

Planning

Before you go   22–25

Getting there   26

Getting around   27–29

Being there   30–33

Before you go

WHEN TO GO

JAN	FEB	MAR	APR	MAY	JUN	JUL	AUG	SEP	OCT	NOV	DEC
6°C	7°C	10°C	13°C	17°C	20°C	22°C	22°C	19°C	14°C	10°C	7°C
43°F	45°F	50°F	55°F	63°F	68°F	72°F	72°F	66°F	57°F	50°F	45°F

🌧️ 🌧️ 🌦️ 🌦️ ☀️ ☀️ ☀️ ☀️ 🌤️ 🌦️ 🌧️ 🌧️

⬤ High season ⬤ Low season

London has a temperate climate. Spring (March to May) has a mixture of sunshine and showers although winter can drag on into March. Summer (June to August) can be unpredictable; clear skies and long hot days one day followed by humid and overcast conditions the next. June has the advantage of long daylight hours; July and August are the hottest and the busiest with long school holidays. September is the official start of autumn, but often retains a summery feel, with October the real start of the season and the colder days setting in during November. Winter (December to February) is generally fairly mild, often wet and windy, any snow or very cold conditions not lasting long. The tip is to be prepared for any eventuality, dress in layers and take an umbrella. For a five-day weather forecast: www.bbc.co.uk/weather

WHAT YOU NEED

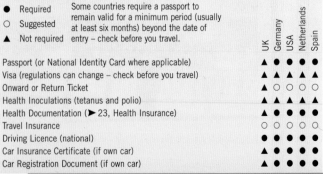

		UK	Germany	USA	Netherlands	Spain
●	Required					
○	Suggested					
▲	Not required					

Some countries require a passport to remain valid for a minimum period (usually at least six months) beyond the date of entry – check before you travel.

	UK	Germany	USA	Netherlands	Spain
Passport (or National Identity Card where applicable)	▲	●	●	●	●
Visa (regulations can change – check before you travel)	▲	▲	▲	▲	▲
Onward or Return Ticket	▲	○	○	○	○
Health Inoculations (tetanus and polio)	▲	▲	▲	▲	▲
Health Documentation (► 23, Health Insurance)	▲	●	●	●	●
Travel Insurance	○	○	○	○	○
Driving Licence (national)	●	●	●	●	●
Car Insurance Certificate (if own car)	▲	●	●	●	●
Car Registration Document (if own car)	▲	●	●	●	●

WEBSITES

Official London tourist office: www.visitlondon.com
Official national tourist office: www.visitbritain.com
Weekly listings: www.timeout.com/london
Transport for London: www.tfl.gov.uk
Society of London Theatre: www.officiallondontheatre.co.uk
Railway enquiries: www.nationalrail.co.uk

TOURIST OFFICES AT HOME

In the USA
7th floor, Suite 701,
551 Fifth Avenue,
New York, NY 10176,
☎ 1-800/462-2748
www.visitbritain.us

In Australia
VisitBritain
Level 3, 32 Walker Street
North Sydney, NSW 2060
☎ 1300 85 85 89
www.visitbritain.com.au

HEALTH INSURANCE

Citizens of the EU and certain other countries receive free or reduced-cost emergency medical treatment in Britain with the relevant documentation (European Health Insurance Card), but private medical insurance is still advised, and is essential for all other visitors.

For emergency dental treatment, find the closest dentist from NHS Direct (0845 4647, www.nhs.uk). Expect to pay about £45 for a consultation and a further £60–£70 for a filling. This can then be claimed back from your insurer.

TIME DIFFERENCES

| GMT | London | Germany | USA (EST) | Netherlands | Spain |
| 12 noon | 12 noon | 1PM | 7AM | 1PM | 1PM |

London is on Greenwich Mean Time (GMT) in winter, but from late March until late October British Summer Time (BST, ie GMT+1) operates.

NATIONAL HOLIDAYS

1 Jan *New Year's Day*
Mar/Apr *Good Friday,*
Easter Monday
First Mon May *May Day*
Bank Holiday
Last Mon May *Spring Bank*
Holiday

Last Mon in Aug *August*
Bank Holiday
25 Dec *Christmas Day*
26 Dec *Boxing Day*

Almost all attractions close on Christmas Day. On other holidays some attractions open, often with reduced hours. There are no general rules regarding the opening times of restaurants and shops, so check before making a special journey.

WHAT'S ON WHEN

January/February

New Year's Day Parade (1 January): this procession of 10,000 performers from around the world (from Westminster Bridge to Berkeley Square) attracts around 500,000 onlookers.

Chinese New Year (late January–early February): human dragons and firecrackers light up Soho's Chinatown.

March/April

(University) Boat Race (late March–early April): Oxford against Cambridge over 6.4km (4 miles) of the Thames from Putney to Chiswick Bridge.

London Marathon (third week in April): some 35,000 runners, from world-class athletes to fancy-dressed 'fun-runners', pound the streets

from Blackheath (Greenwich) to the Mall in front of a sea of 750,000 cheering spectators.

May

Baishakhi Mela (mid-May): Europe's largest Asian street festival celebrating the Bengali New Year with food stalls, parades and rickshaw rides in and around Brick Lane.

RHS Chelsea Flower Show (late May): the world's best horticultural show, held in the grounds of the Royal Hospital, Chelsea.

June/July

Trooping the Colour (second Saturday in June): an inspection and parade of the guards honours the Sovereign's official birthday. Watch the procession in the Mall.

Wimbledon Tennis Championship (last week June, first week July): you can line up for early rounds but it's advance ticket-holders for the latter stages.

BBC Proms (mid-July to mid-September): Britain's best-loved classical concert series occupies the Royal Albert Hall for two months.

August

Notting Hill Carnival (August bank holiday weekend): the Caribbean comes to London with the biggest street festival in Europe.

September

Thames Festival: a celebration of the River Thames between Westminster and Tower bridges, culminating in spectacular fireworks.

October

Punch & Judy Festival (first Sunday in October): a celebration of an English tradition in Covent Garden's North Hall.

November–December

State Opening of Parliament (late November to early December): pomp and ceremony as the Queen arrives at Parliament in the Gold State Coach.

London-to-Brighton Veteran Car Run (first Sunday in November): a great spectacle as Hyde Park is crammed with 500 pre-1950s vehicles. The world's oldest motor event.

Lord Mayor's Show (second Saturday in November): London's 800-year-old street parade, from Mansion House to the Royal Courts of Justice. Fireworks at 5pm.

Christmas Lights (mid-November to early January): Regent Street and Oxford Street glow with the latest festive creations.

Getting there

BY AIR

London Heathrow Airport

25km (15.5 miles) to city centre

15 minutes

50–60 minutes

60 minutes

London Gatwick Airport

48km (30 miles) to city centre

30 minutes

90 minutes

65–75 minutes

There are direct flights to London from all over the world. London has two main airports, Heathrow and Gatwick, with smaller airports at Luton, Stansted and London City (Docklands). There are train links to Paris and Brussels, and good road links to the Channel ports.

BY TRAIN

Visitors from Europe can come by train through the Channel Tunnel. Foot passengers can use the Eurostar trains (☎ 08705 186186; www.eurostar.com), which offer a direct link between Paris or Brussels and London (St Pancras International) in under three hours. The car-carrying train Eurotunnel (☎ 08705 35 35 35; www.eurotunnel.com) operates between Calais in France and Folkestone in England and takes around 35 minutes.

OTHER OPTIONS

Passenger and car ferries operate from Ireland, France, Belgium, Netherlands, Germany, Scandinavia and Spain (www.ferries.co.uk). Trains link the arrival ports directly with London.

Long-distance coaches generally arrive at Victoria Coach Station close to London Victoria main line and underground rail station (☎ 08450 130 130; www.nationalexpress.com).

Getting around

PUBLIC TRANSPORT

Internal flights Internal flights link Northern Ireland, Scotland, Wales and the regions with many of London's airports. London City Airport is in Docklands, about 10km (6 miles) from the City financial district.

Trains London is at the centre of Britain's rail network, with lines going out from its principal stations – north from King's Cross, northwest from Euston, east from Liverpool Street, west from Paddington, southwest from Waterloo, south from Victoria and southeast from Charing Cross. A comprehensive suburban rail network complements the underground.

Buses London's red double-decker buses cover the capital in a network of services. A red bus stop symbol on a white background indicates that the bus must stop (unless it is full); otherwise you must hail the bus by putting out an arm. Instead of buying single tickets, buy a Visitor Oyster Card to save time and money. Use it for all London underground, buses, Docklands Light Railway and trams. Details at www.tfl.gov.uk

River transport There are regular services from Westminster to the Tower of London, Greenwich and Docklands. Sightseeing boats are frequent and popular, and offer some of London's most memorable views.

Underground The underground, or Tube, is the quickest way to get around London. Maps are on display at stations, on platforms and on the trains, and lines are named and colour-coded. Tube trains run from around 5:30am to around midnight.

TAXIS

London's black cabs are driven by licensed 'cabbies'. Hail them when the yellow TAXI sign is lit. A meter records the fare. The alternative is a 'mini-cab', which you must always book in advance (☎ 020 7222 1234).

DRIVING

- The British drive on the left side of the road.
- Seat belts must be worn in front seats at all times and in rear seats where fitted.
- Random breath tests may be carried out, especially late at night. The limit is 35 micrograms of alcohol in 100ml of breath (blood alcohol content 0.05%). Never drive under the influence of alcohol.
- Fuel is sold in litres and is available as unleaded, lead replacement petrol (LRP) or diesel. In central London, fuel stations are few and far between but there are many open 24 hours on the main roads leading away from the centre and in the suburbs.
- Speed limits are as follows:
  On motorways and dual carriageways: 112kph (70mph)
  On main roads: 80–100kph (50–60mph)
  On minor roads: 50–65kph (30–40mph)

TRAFFIC CONGESTION

The average vehicle speed in London today is 16kph (10mph), not much faster than it was in 1900! Some 7 million people per day choose to ride on the bus and tube networks. Congestion charges in the 'inner ring' of the city (£8 per day; exemptions for disabled and alternative fuel vehicles) are now in force on weekdays (7am–6pm) to ease the traffic problems.

CAR RENTAL

The leading international car rental companies have offices at all London airports and you can reserve a car in advance. Local companies offer competitive rates and will deliver a car to the airport .

FARES AND CONCESSIONS

Students and senior citizens Holders of an International Student Identity Card (ISIC) and senior citizens (usually over 60) can obtain some discounts on travel and entrance fees.

The London Pass This is a pass to over 55 top attractions as well as an option for travel on buses, tubes and trains. The aim of the pass is to fast track and save money at selected major attractions. The pass is valid for either one, two, three or six days. It also offers discounts on restaurants and leisure activities. For further information www.londonpass.com

Being there

TOURIST OFFICES

Main office
Britain and London Visitor Centre,
1 Lower Regent Street
☎ 0870 156 6366

Alternative office
City of London,
St Paul's Churchyard

Other information points include: the bright orange Holborn Information Kiosk, Kingsway (outside Holborn Tube station), the Travel Information Centres at Euston Railway Station, Liverpool Street Railway Station, Piccadilly Circus Station and Victoria Station. There is also an information centre at the underground station that serves Heathrow's terminals 1, 2 and 3. You can also get help from any of the 300 or so 'London Ambassadors', wearing badges with the Visit London and *i* logos.

MONEY

Britain's currency is the pound sterling (£), issued in notes of £5, £10, £20 and £50. There are 100 pennies or pence (p) to each pound and coins come in denominations of 1p, 2p, 5p, 10p, 20p, 50p, £1 and £2.

Travellers' cheques may be accepted by some hotels, shops and restaurants. Travellers' cheques in pounds are the most convenient. Exchange offices are common in central London, but they often offer poorer rates of exchange. Credit and debit cards are widely accepted.

Automatic teller machines (ATMs) are widely available throughout London but be aware of security when using them.

TIPS/GRATUITIES

Yes ✓   No ✗

Restaurants (if service not included)	✓	10–12.5%
Tour Guides	✓	£1–£2
Cafés/bars	✗	
Taxis	✓	10%
Chambermaids	✓	50p–£1 per day
Porters	✓	50p–£1

POSTAL SERVICES

Post offices are open Mon–Fri 9–5:30, Sat 9–12. The exception is Trafalgar Square Post Office, 24–28 William IV Street, open Mon–Fri 8:30–6:30 (Tue from 9:15am), Sat 9–5:30.

TELEPHONES

The traditional red phone boxes are now rare; instead, kiosks come in a wide variety of different designs and colours, depending on which phone company is operating them.

Coin-operated telephones take 10p, 20p, 50p and £1 coins, but card-operated phones are often more convenient. Phonecards are available from many shops. Hotel phones are very expensive. To call the operator dial 100.

International dialling codes

From London to:
Germany: 00 49
USA: 00 1
Canada: 00 1
Netherlands: 00 31
Spain: 00 34

Emergency telephone numbers

Police: 999
Fire: 999
Ambulance: 999

You can also dial 112 to be connected to the same services

EMBASSIES AND CONSULATES

Germany ☎ 020 7824 1300
USA ☎ 020 7499 9000

Netherlands ☎ 020 7590 3200
Spain ☎ 020 7235 5555

HEALTH ADVICE

Weather Although London is not renowned for its sunny weather, the sun can be strong in July and August, when many Londoners take to the parks to sunbathe. Some sights involve being outdoors for prolonged periods: 'cover up', apply sunscreen and drink plenty of water.

Drugs Prescription and non-prescription drugs and medicines are available from chemists/ pharmacies. Pharmacists can advise on medication for common ailments. London's only 24-hour chemist is Zafash, 233–235 Old Brompton Road (☎ 020 7373 2798; www.zafash.com).

Safe water Tap water is safe to drink. Mineral water is widely available but is often expensive, particularly in restaurants.

PERSONAL SAFETY
London is generally a safe city and police officers are often seen on the beat (walking the streets) in the central areas. They are usually friendly and very approachable.

To help prevent crime:
● Do not carry more cash than you need
● Beware of pickpockets in markets, on the underground, in tourist sights or crowded places
● Avoid walking alone in dark alleys at night

ELECTRICITY
The power supply in Britain is 240 volts.

Sockets only accept three (square)-pin plugs, so an adaptor is needed for Continental and US appliances. A transformer is needed for appliances operating on 110–120 volts.

OPENING HOURS

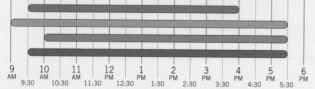

The times shown are traditional opening hours. Many shops in the West End open for longer hours and also on Sunday. High Street banks are open Saturday morning and exchange offices are open daily until late. Smaller museums may close one day a week. Lunch usually is taken between 12 and 2:30 and dinner from 7 until 11.

LANGUAGE

Every city has its own vocabulary for everyday places and objects. Here are just a few expressions that you might hear or read.

betting shop, bookie	Legal place to gamble on horses, football etc
bitter	Popular style of draft beer (as in 'pint of bitter')
Buck House	Buckingham Palace, the Queen's home
cabbie	Cab or taxi driver
The City	Specifically the square mile that is London's business district
Cockney	Someone from the East End of London, traditionally 'born within the sound of Bow Bells', a church in the city
Cockney	a dialect spoken by Cockneys, with its rhyming slang
dustman, dustbin	Refuse/garbage collector, refuse/garbage bin
The East End	East of the City; traditionally the poorer part of London
fiver, tenner	£5, £10 note
football	Association football; rarely 'soccer'
grand	A thousand pounds
hole-in-the-wall	Slang for an ATM or cash machine
local	A pub frequented by people living or working nearby
Lord's	North London's world-famous cricket ground
Marks, M and S	Marks & Spencer: popular High Street store
mini-cab	Alternative to black taxis; must be licensed to be legal
off-licence	Shop selling beer, wine, spirits
Number 10	Where the Prime Minister lives (10 Downing Street)
Oyster Card	The electronic travel card now widely used
plastic	Credit or debit card (as in 'Can I pay with plastic?')
quid	£1 (money)
The River	Always refers to the River Thames
The Tube	The underground train service
The West End	Central London, round Piccadilly Circus: the theatres, clubs, shops

Best places to see

British Museum	36–37
Covent Garden	38–39
Houses of Parliament (Palace of Westminster)	40–41
National Gallery	42–43
Natural History Museum	44–45
St Paul's Cathedral	46–47
Science Museum	48–49
Tower of London	50–51
V&A	52–53
Westminster Abbey	54–55

1 British Museum

www.britishmuseum.org

The British Museum holds what is probably the greatest collection of antiquities in the world, and is also the country's most visited cultural attraction.

Founded in 1753 from the collection of Sir Hans Sloane, the BM (as it is known to its regulars) has occupied its present site since 1852. The world's oldest museum has 4km (2.5 miles) of galleries displaying objects representing almost every aspect of international cultural history. The glass-roofed Great Court, designed by Sir Norman Foster and opened to the public in December 2000, is now Europe's largest covered square.

The following are just a few of the BM's greatest and most popular treasures. Pick up a floor plan to locate them: starting on the ground floor, the sculptures from the Parthenon (the Elgin Marbles) are widely held to be the greatest works of their kind from ancient Greece. The adjacent Nereid Monument, from Xanthos, Turkey, is a striking reconstructed temple. For more breathtaking sculptures on a monumental scale see the Assyrian human-headed winged bulls of Khorsabad. The museum boasts the greatest collection of Egyptology outside Cairo, including the famous Rosetta Stone, which enabled scholars to decipher the meaning of hieroglyphics. Just as memorable and equally worthwhile are the Oriental Collection (particularly the Indian sculptures) and the Mexican Gallery, both of which contain outstandingly beautiful works of art.

On the upper floor follow the crowds to the macabre Egyptian mummies and the preserved un-mummified body of 'Ginger'. In the Prehistoric and Romano-British sections, highlights include Lindow Man, the Sutton Hoo Treasure, the Mildenhall Treasure and the Lewis Chessmen. The Clocks and Watches collection is one of the finest in the world. Be there on the hour when the clocks chime in unison. Easily overlooked among the antiquities from Greece and Rome is the Portland Vase, a 2,000-year-old glass vessel.

✚ 15L ✉ Great Russell Street, Bloomsbury ☎ 020 7323 8000 🕐 Main museum Sat–Wed 10–5:30, Thu, Fri 10–8:30; Great Court Mon–Wed, Sun 9–6, Thu–Sat 9am–11pm. Reading Room: daily 10–5:30. Closed 24–26 Dec, 1 Jan, Good Fri 🎟 Free 🍴 Café (£), restaurant (££) 🚇 Holborn, Tottenham Court Road, Russell Square 🚌 New Oxford Street 1, 7, 8, 19, 25, 38, 55, 98, 242; Tottenham Court Road northbound and Gower Street southbound 10, 14, 24, 29, 73, 134, 390; Southampton Row 59, 68, 91, 168, 188

2 Covent Garden

www.coventgardenlondonuk.com

London's most popular open space is thronged with shoppers and sightseers by day, and with theatregoers and revellers by night.

Covent Garden piazza was laid out in the Italian style in 1630 by Inigo Jones. Initially it was a very fashionable address, but from 1670 onwards, with the advent of the main London fruit, flower and vegetable market, it deteriorated and developed into a notorious red-light area. In 1830 its handsome centrepiece iron and glass hall was erected and the market continued trading at Covent Garden until 1974, when, finally defeated by transport logistics, it moved south of the River Thames to Vauxhall. The site was then developed as a pedestrianized area, accommodating dozens of small shops and restaurants. The fruit and

vegetable stalls were replaced with the Apple Market, home to crafts, jewellery, clothing, accessories and antiques and collectables.

Today, only some arcading and St Paul's Church remain of the original piazza. By the church portico street performers (licensed by the Covent Garden authorities) entertain large crowds daily. It was here, in 1662, that England's first ever Punch and Judy show was staged. St Paul's is known as the Actors' Church because of the large number of commemorative memorials (and graves) of screen and stage stars it holds. It is well worth a look inside and its garden is a remarkably peaceful oasis amid the general hubbub.

Other major attractions include the London Transport Museum (➤ 142) and the 150-year-old Royal Opera House (➤ 156), home of the Royal Opera and the Royal Ballet.

 16J 🚇 Covent Garden

3 Houses of Parliament (Palace of Westminster)

www.parliament.uk

The home of the Mother of Parliaments, and a masterpiece of Victorian Gothic, has over 1,000 rooms and the world's most famous clock tower.

The Houses of Parliament, seat of British government, date back to 1087, when William the Conqueror's son built his Palace of Westminster on this site. It evolved into a parliament around the mid-13th century and continued to be used as a royal palace until 1512, when Henry VIII moved his court to Whitehall. In 1834 a disastrous fire burned everything above ground (with the exception of

Westminster Hall, the cloisters and the Jewel Tower), and so construction began of the building that you see today. The principal architect was Charles Barry, though the flamboyant Gothic decorative touches are the work of his assistant, Augustus Pugin. By 1860, some 20 years later than planned and around £1.4 million over budget, it was virtually complete. The best-known part of the Houses is the clock tower, referred to as Big Ben – though to be precise this is the name of the great 13-ton bell that chimes every hour. After dark a light above the clock face indicates when Parliament is 'sitting' (when it is in session).

The modern Houses of Parliament divide principally into two debating chambers. The House of Commons consists of Members of Parliament (MPs), the elected representatives of the British people. Their functions are legislation and (as opposition) government scrutiny. The House of Lords is a body of unelected peers who examine proposed legislation from the Commons and also act as the highest Appeal Court in the land.

✚ 12D ✉ Cromwell Green, St Margaret Street
☎ Information Office 020 7219 3000 (Commons), 020 7219 3107 (Lords) ⏺ The public may attend debates when the Houses are sitting ✋ Free; summer tours expensive
Ⓜ Westminster 🚌 3, 11, 12, 24, 53, 87, 88, 148, 159, 211, 453 🚆 Waterloo

4 National Gallery

www.nationalgallery.org.uk

Home to one of the finest and most extensive collections of Western European paintings in the world, the National Gallery houses over 2,300 paintings.

The collection progresses chronologically, with the oldest paintings in the Sainsbury Wing. Among the 13th- to 15th-century masterpieces is *Venus and Mars* by Botticelli. *The Doge* by Giovanni Bellini is widely considered the greatest Venetian portrait. Less famous but equally worthwhile are *The Wilton Diptych* (by an unknown artist), *The Battle of San Romano* by Uccello, *The Baptism of Christ* by Piero della Francesca and *The Arnolfini Portrait* by Jan van Eyck.

The 16th-century Renaissance masterpieces in the West Wing include *The Virgin and Child* cartoon by Leonardo da Vinci and the unfinished *Entombment* by Michelangelo. Two famous mythology paintings are *Bacchus and Ariadne* by Titian and *Allegory with Venus and Cupid* by Bronzino. More 'worldly' masterpieces include Holbein's *Ambassadors* and *Pope Julius II* by Raphael.

The North Wing deals with the 17th century. Among its 15 or so Rembrandts is the sorrowful *Self Portrait at the Age of 63* (that same

year he died a pauper). Contrast this with the pompous *Equestrian Portrait of Charles I* by Van Dyck, and the charming *Le Chapeau de Paille* (Straw Hat) portrait by Rubens. *Young Woman Standing at a Virginal* by Vermeer, *The Rokeby Venus* by Velázquez and *Enchanted Castle* by Claude are also worth seeking out.

The East Wing (1700–1900) contains a whole host of popular favourites: *Sunflowers* by Van Gogh; *Bathers at Asnières* by Seurat; *Gare St-Lazare* by Monet; and from the British school, *The Hay Wain* by Constable and *Fighting Temeraire* by Turner.

✚ 15J ✉ Trafalgar Square ☎ 020 7747 2885 🕐 Daily 10–6 (Fri until 9). Closed 24–26 Dec, 1 Jan 🖐 Free 🍴 Café (£), brasserie (££) 🚇 Charing Cross, Leicester Square, Embankment 🚌 3, 6, 9, 11, 12, 13, 15, 23, 24, 29, 53, 77a, 88, 91, 139, 159, 176, 453 🚉 Charing Cross

5 Natural History Museum

www.nhm.ac.uk

A family favourite, where dinosaurs roar back to life, an erathquake shakes the ground and creepy-crawlies make the flesh tingle.

Surveying the diplodocus skeleton that dominates Central Hall is the marble statue of Charles Darwin. To coincide with the 150th anniversary of the publication of his theory of evolution, the new Darwin Centre opened in 2009. The most exciting addition to the Museum since 1881, this eight-storey glass and steel building boasts state-of-the-art exhibits, where visitors can watch scientists at work in their laboratories.

To help you get around this vast museum, follow the colour-coding. Orange is dedicated to Darwin, with an exit to the outdoor wildlife garden (Apr–Oct). Blue is all about dinosaurs and mammals, while Green covers birds, bugs, fossils and minerals. It includes another tribute to Darwin, called TREE, an artwork inspired by Darwin's 'tree of life' diagram. The former Geological Museum, now the Red Zone, is all about the planet itself.

Although dinosaurs are at the top of every child's list of must-sees, there are other heavyweights. A model of a blue whale measures 28m (92ft), alongside a real 25m (82ft) long skeleton. At the other end of the spectrum are the insects in the Creepy Crawlies exhibit. Scientists seem to love insects and fossils. In fact, the fossil insect

collection includes
Rhyniognatha hirsti,
the world's oldest
fossil insect, dating
back 400 million years.

The Human Biology
section fascinates,
with its explanations of
how the body works.
And all this is set in the
1880 neo-Gothic
cathedral-like building,
with its extraordinary
brickwork, sculptures
and carvings. There are
regular tours, and for
children, self-guided
trails using backpacks
and booklets.

✚ 3C ✉ Cromwell Road
(Life Galleries), Exhibition
Road (Earth Galleries)
☎ 020 7942 5000
🕐 Daily 10–5:50. Last
admission 5:30. Closed
24–26 Dec 🎫 Free
🍽 Restaurant (££) and
cafés (£) 🚇 South
Kensington 🚌 14, 49, 70,
74, 345, 360, 414, C1
❓ Explore tour: daily 45
mins long. Reserve on the
day at the information desk
or call 020 7942 5011. Free

6 St Paul's Cathedral

www.stpauls.co.uk

The Mother Church of the Diocese of London and the supreme work of Sir Christopher Wren, one of the world's great architects.

Work began on the present St Paul's Cathedral after the Great Fire of 1666 had destroyed its predecessor, Old St Paul's. Its foundation stone was laid by Christopher Wren in 1675 and after 35 years of sweat and toil (during which time Wren's salary was halved as punishment for slow progress) it was completed in 1710. Take time to enjoy the magnificent west front before entering the church. Inside it is surprisingly light and airy, largely as a result of the use of plain glass windows (much favoured by Wren), which were installed to replace the old stained glass ones that were destroyed during World War II.

Go past the huge monument to the Duke of Wellington and stop in the middle of the transepts to look skywards to the wonderful dome – one of the three largest in the world. Move on to the choir, the most lavishly decorated part of the church, and don't miss the scorch-marked statue of John Donne (poet and Dean of Old St Paul's). This is one of London's very few monuments to survive the Great Fire of 1666.

Descend to the crypt, where you will find the tombs of some of Britain's greatest heroes, including the Duke of Wellington and Lord Nelson, and, of course, Christopher Wren himself. Return to the church and begin the ascent to the galleries. The justifiably famous Whispering Gallery, whose remarkable acoustics will carry a whisper quite audibly from one side to the other, is perched 30m (98ft) above the floor. Finally, after a total of 530 steps, you will reach the Golden Gallery, where

you will be rewarded with one of the finest views in all London. Return to the cathedral floor and contemplate William Holman Hunt's uplifting masterpiece, *The Light of the World*.

✚ 20K ✉ St Paul's Churchyard ☎ 020 7236 4128 🕔 Mon–Sat 8:30–4:30 (last admission 4) 🎫 Expensive, includes cathedral, crypt and climbing galleries 🍴 Restaurant (£); café in crypt (£) 🚇 St Paul's 🚌 4, 11, 15, 23, 26, 100 🚉 St Paul's, City Thameslink ❓ Self-guided audio tours, 90-min guided tours

7 Science Museum

www.sciencemuseum.org.uk

Trace the 250-year development of the modern industrial world, delve into the history of medicine, blast off to outer space and enjoy the motionride simulators.

The Science Museum is one of the world's finest collections of its kind. It is a huge undertaking, and you can't hope to see everything here in a single visit. On the other hand there are so many pieces that are landmarks of industrial history, technological milestones, works of art, or just amazing objects in their own right, there really is something that everyone can identify with and admire.

To see the best of the collection in one visit buy the excellent museum guidebook, which will navigate you through the 'must-see' exhibits such as Stephenson's *Rocket*, Edison's early lamps, Crick and Watson's DNA model, the prototype computer (the dauntingly huge Babbage's Difference Engine), the Apollo 10 Command module, the first iron lung and many other famous technological landmarks.

The Science Museum is famous for its pioneering interactive hands-on areas and adults with children should start with the most popular hands-on display, Launchpad. Here youngsters can discover how machines and gadgets work. Other family favourites include the Flight Galleries, featuring a whole array of historic aircraft, many of them slung dramatically from the ceiling. For sheer spectacle it's hard to beat the Energy Hall, where some of the great beam-and-steam behemoths that powered the Industrial Revolution still push and thrust their mighty workings.

The fifth-floor Science and the Art of Medicine displays range from ancient medicine to the very latest discoveries, from Roman tweezers to face transplants and artificial noses.

✚ 4D ✉ Exhibition Road ☎ 0870 870 4868 🕐 Daily 10–6. Closed 24–26 Dec 👤 Free 🍴 Restaurants (£), café (£), picnic areas 🚇 South Kensington 🚌 9, 10, 14, 49, 52, 70, 74, 345, 360, 414, 430, C1 ❓ IMAX cinema (moderate); simulators (inexpensive)

8 Tower of London

www.hrp.org.uk

London's foremost historical site, the Tower has served as castle, palace, prison, arsenal, jewel house and site of execution over its 900-year lifespan.

The oldest part of the Tower of London is the great central keep. Known as the White Tower, it was begun by William I in the 1080s to intimidate his

ENTRY TO THE TRAITORS GATE

newly conquered subjects; the rest of the fortifications took on their present shape in the late 13th and early 14th centuries.

Begin with an hour-long, highly entertaining guided walk led by one of the Tower's traditionally dressed Yeoman Warders (Beefeaters). They gleefully relate stories of imprisonment, torture and intrigue – later on you can check out the Prisoners of the Tower exhibition for further gruesome details – while taking you past a few of the 20 towers, the famous ravens ('only so long as they stay will the White Tower stand'), Traitors' Gate and the execution site of Tower Green. Here, among others, Henry VIII's wives Anne Boleyn and Catherine Howard lost their heads.

After visiting the adjacent Chapel of St Peter ad Vincula, head for the highlights for most visitors: the Jewel House and the White Tower. Both are well worth the wait.

The former houses the Crown Jewels, many of which date back to the 17th-century Restoration period and are still used by the present Queen and royal family. The White Tower is home to the beautiful 11th-century Chapel of St John. Also highly recommended is a visit to the restored rooms of the medieval palace.

✚ 23J ✉ Tower of London ☎ 0844 482 7777
🕐 Mar–Oct Tue–Sat 9–5:30, Sun, Mon 10–5:30 (last admission 5); Nov–Feb Tue–Sat 9–4:30, Sun–Mon 10–4:30 (last admission 4). Closed 24–26 Dec, 1 Jan ✋ Expensive
🍴 Café (£), restaurant (£) 🚇 Tower Hill 🚌 15, 42, 78, 100, D1 🚃 Fenchurch Street, London Bridge ❓ To save time, buy tickets in advance online. Audio guides available

V&A

www.vam.ac.uk

The V&A is Britain's national museum of art and design, and contains the greatest collection of decorative arts in the world.

The Victoria and Albert Museum was founded in 1852 with the objective of exhibiting the world's very best examples of design and applied arts in order to inspire students and craftspeople. It has subsequently grown to include an astonishing and immense diversity of objects, so try to link up with one of the six free daily tours (60 min), lead by docents, who are both enthusiastic and knowledgeable.

Perhaps the V&A's greatest treasures are the Raphael Cartoons, seven huge tapestry designs that have become even more famous than the actual tapestries themselves (which hang in the Sistine Chapel in Rome). While on the ground floor, don't miss the Italian Renaissance

sculptures; the Cast Courts, full-size plaster casts of fascinating European masterpieces including Trajan's Column and Michelangelo's *David*; and the Morris, Poynter and Gamble Rooms, the V&A's original refreshment rooms and themselves masterpieces of Victorian decoration.

Dip into the treasures of the Orient from China, Japan, the Muslim world and India – don't miss Tippoo's Tiger, one of the museum's most famous pieces – and the Fashion collections.

Changes made since 2005 have made the V&A even better: the ten galleries telling the story of European art and design between AD300 and AD1600, the Jameel Gallery's Islamic treasures, the Gilbert Collection's hoard of gold and silver, and the Theatre and Performance Galleries, with memorabilia and film clips from the world of opera, drama and pop music.

✚ 4D ✉ Entrances on Exhibition Road, Cromwell Road ☎ 020 7942 2000; 0844 209 1770 for advance tickets ⏰ Sat–Thu 10–5:45, Fri 10–10. Closed 24–26, 31 Dec, 1 Jan ♿ Free ⬛ Excellent cafés (£) and restaurant (££) on premises ⬛ South Kensington ⬛ C1, 14, 74, 414 stop outside Cromwell Road entrance ❓ Tours: free introductory tours daily (lasting 1 hour) hourly 10:30–3:30

10 Westminster Abbey

www.westminster-abbey.org

The coronation site of British royalty, the last resting place of kings, queens and celebrities, this architectural triumph is awash with history.

Westminster Abbey was founded *c*1050 by Edward the Confessor, who was the first king to be buried here. William the Conqueror was crowned king in the abbey on Christmas Day in 1066 and so began a tradition that was last re-enacted in 1953 when the coronation of the present monarch, Queen Elizabeth II, took place here.

The present building dates mostly from the 13th century and the reign of Henry III. The nave is full of graves and monuments, none more famous

than the Tomb of the Unknown Warrior, that represents the 765,000 British servicemen killed in World War I, though the real glory of the abbey lies beyond the sumptuously carved and gilded choir screen (by which Isaac Newton and Charles Darwin lie) in the Royal Chapels. Here you will find the coronation chair and the often magnificent tombs of dozens of royals.

The abbey's *tour de force* lies at its easternmost point;

Henry VII's Lady Chapel, built between 1503 and 1519, with its sublime fan-vaulting. In the south transept is the famous Poets' Corner where many celebrated writers, musicians and artists are honoured.

Try to see the beautiful abbey precinct that includes the cloisters, the Westminster Abbey Museum (with contemporary royal wax effigies), the Chapter House and the Pyx ('money chest') Chamber with its medieval tiled floor.

➕ 11D ✉ Dean's Yard, Broad Sanctuary ☎ Abbey 020 7654 4900 🕐 Cloisters daily 8–6; abbey Mon–Fri 9:30–4:30, Sat 9:30–1:30. Last admission 1 hour before closing time. No sightseeing on Sun. Pyx Chamber, Chapter House and museum daily 10:30–3:30 🖐 Cloisters free; abbey expensive, includes Chapter House, museum, Pyx Chamber 🍴 Coffee stands outside abbey and in cloister 🚇 Westminster, St James's Park 🚌 3, 11, 24, 53, 77a, 159, 211 ❓ Guided tours: Apr–Sep Mon–Fri 10, 10:30, 11, 2, 2:30; Sat 10, 10:30, 11; Oct–Mar Mon–Fri 10:30, 11, 2, 2:30; Sat 10:30, 11 ☎ Reserve tours in advance 020 7654 4832 🖐 Moderate; audio tour available Mon–Fri 9:30–3:30, Sat 9:30–1:30 🖐 Inexpensive–moderate

Best things to do

Good places to have lunch   58–59

Top activities   60–61

A walk around the Docklands   62–63

Stunning views   64–65

Great traditional pubs   66–67

Places to take the children   68–69

Best shopping areas   70–71

Good places to have lunch

Ba Shan (£–££)

Order authentic Sichuan street snacks in this modern version of a traditional Chinese café in Soho.

✉ 24 Romilly Street ☎ 020 7287 3266

Butler's Wharf Chop House (££)

British food combined with great views of the river.

✉ Butler's Wharf Building, 36E Shad Thames ☎ 020 7403 3403

Café in the Crypt (£)

This oasis of calm will provide a welcome break from the frenzied activity of Trafalgar Square. Good salads, soups, sandwiches and light meals.

✉ St Martin-in-the-Fields, Duncannon Street ☎ 020 7766 1158

Fountain Restaurant (££)

Informal brasserie in posh Fortnum and Mason store.

✉ Jermyn Street entrance ☎ 0845 602 5694

The Gun (£–££)

Waterside gastropub in Docklands, serving stylish pub grub.

✉ 27 Coldharbour ☎ 020 7515 5222

Inn the Park (££)

Contemporary restaurant in the heart of St James's Park.

✉ St James's Park, near Admiralty Arch ☎ 020 7451 9999

J Sheekey (£–££)

A West End theatrical institution: fish and seafood with a modern twist.

✉ 28–32 St Martin's Court ☎ 020 7240 2565

Northbank (£–££)

By the Millennium Bridge, overlooking Tate Modern, this serves well-priced Modern English dishes: cheese and onion tart, and herby sausages.

✉ 1 Paul's Walk ☎ 020 7329 9299

Portrait Restaurant (£–££)

Food matches views from the National Portrait Gallery's rooftop restaurant.

✉ St Martin's Place, Trafalgar Square ☎ 020 7312 2490

World Food Café (£)

An organic health food eatery set in a courtyard overlooking Neal's Yard.

✉ 14 Neal's Yard, Covent Garden ☎ 020 7379 0298

Top activities

Take a cycle tour with the London Bicycle Tour Company. Guided tours start near the London Eye (www.londonbicycle.com).

Take a spin in a rickshaw. Let someone else do the hard work. Hail one outside Covent Garden Tube station.

Picnic in one of the big parks on sandwiches and a bottle of wine.

Go rowing on the Serpentine in the heart of Hyde Park. Rent a rowing boat or a pedalo on this 11-ha (28-acre) lake.

Go riding in Hyde Park. Another way to enjoy the park is on horseback. Hire from Briggs Stables (tel: 020 7723 2813).

Go ice-skating – on small artificial rinks in winter outside the Tower of London, Somerset House and the Natural History Museum.

Watch fireworks after the Thames Festival (mid-September), Lord Mayor's Show (November) and New Year's Eve. But the biggest night of the year is Bonfire Night, on or near November 5.

Enjoy afternoon tea in a grand West End hotel.

Visit a market such as Camden or Portobello or Borough Market.

Watch the Changing of the Guard at Buckingham Palace (► 76–78). Get there early to see a 500-year-old tradition.

a walk around the Docklands

On this walk see where 'new' London stands on the old city's footprint. St Katharine Docks (▶ 104–105) marks the start of London's Docklands. The area goes to sleep at the weekend so it is best to do this walk during the working week.

Follow signs for St Katharine's Way and the Thames Path that follow the river, sometimes overlooking the water, sometimes running behind old warehouses that are now converted into apartments.

Along Wapping High Street are historic pubs (The Town of Ramsgate, The Captain Kidd) as well as the 200-year-old Marine Police force. Handsome Georgian homes line Wapping Pier Head's leafy square.

At New Crane Wharf, bear left on Garnet Street. On a fine day, turn right on Wapping Wall for The Prospect of Whitby, yet another historic waterside pub. Otherwise, continue on Garnet Street over the iron bridge, following signs for Shadwell DLR (Docklands Light Railway) overground station. To get there, cross The Highway at the traffic lights and walk up Dellow Street. Take a train (destination Lewisham) to Island Gardens.

As you ride high above the rooftops, see how Docklands has changed, thanks to gleaming post-modernist buildings, such as Canary Wharf and the O_2 Arena.

Get out at Island Garden.

Just a few steps away, are views across the river to Greenwich.

From here you have a choice: either continue on the DLR from Island Gardens to the Cutty Sark stop in Greenwich and enjoy 'a walk around Greenwich' (▶ 160–161) or, take the DLR back to Canary Wharf.

Explore this new, bustling business district with its shops, restaurants and waterside pubs. You can then return to central London from Canary Wharf underground station.

Distance Walk approximately 3km (2 miles)
Time 3–4 hours (walk and DLR), including stops
Start point St Katharine Docks, Tower Hill ✚ 24H
End point Canary Wharf
Lunch Prospect of Whitby (▶ 109) or various options at Canary Wharf

Stunning views

Boat trip from Westminster Pier to Greenwich to see how London has grown since Roman times.

Greenwich Park, Royal Observatory (► 159).

London Hilton on Park Lane has 360° views from the Galvin at Windows bar on the 28th floor.

London Eye (► 118–119).

Monument (► 98).

Oxo Tower (► 119).

Parliament Hill (► 163).

St Paul's Cathedral (► 46–47).

Top deck of a double decker bus.

Tower Bridge (► 106–107).

Tate Modern has terrific views of St Paul's Cathedral and the river from its Level 7 café and bar (► 123).

Waterloo Bridge (► 19).

Great traditional pubs

The Grenadier
Fine 18th-century Knightsbridge mews pub. Largely undiscovered by tourists.
✉ Old Barrack Yard, Wilton Row

Jerusalem Tavern
Built in 1720, this traditional pub serves excellent food and beer.
✉ 55 Britton Street, Clerkenwell

The Lamb
Dickens reputedly enjoyed a drink here. Unspoiled Victorian gem serving good food and beer.
✉ 94 Lamb's Conduit Street

Lamb and Flag
The oldest pub in Covent Garden, with plenty of character, simple but tasty food and a good selection of beers.
✉ 33 Rose Street, Covent Garden

Red Lion
This classic, with its mahogany bar and cut-glass mirrors, dates back to 1821. Pub grub includes bangers and mash (sausages and mashed potatoes) and steak and ale pie. Closed Sundays.
✉ 2 Duke of York Street, off Jermyn Street

Salisbury
Bustling, beautifully preserved Victorian pub in the heart of Theatreland.
✉ 90 St Martin's Lane, Covent Garden

Seven Stars
Tucked away behind the Royal Courts of Justice, this 400-year-old pub survived the Great Fire of London. Good food, range of ales.
✉ 53 Carey Street, off Chancery Lane

Places to take the children

Cartoon Museum
Close to the British Museum, this is a real hands-on museum. As well as comics such as *The Beano* and *Dandy*, kids can have a go up in the Young Artists' Gallery, where paper and pencils are provided. Regular animation and cartooning workshops.

✉ 35 Little Russell Street ☎ 020 7580 8155 🖐 Moderate, free to under-18s Ⓣ Holborn

Golden Hinde
On board an accurate replica vessel, travel back to the 16th century with sailors in Tudor costumes to hear about naval warfare, weapons and the rigours of life at sea, and learn about Sir Francis Drake's voyage around the world.

✉ Golden Hinde, St Mary Overie Dock, beside Southwark Cathedral ☎ 0870 0118 700 🕐 Mon–Sat 10–5:30, Sun 10:30–5 Ⓣ London Bridge 🖐 Moderate

Hamleys
With 250 years of history, Hamleys flagship store is one of the most famous toystores in the world. Always busy, this magnet to parents and children boasts seven floors of fun, from model kits to stuffed toys, dolls to action figures.

✉ 188–196 Regent Street ☎ 0870 333 2455 🕐 Mon–Fri 10–8, Sat 9–8, Sun 12–6 Ⓣ Oxford Circus, Piccadilly Circus

Little Angel Theatre
Known as the 'home of British puppetry', this 100-seat theatre has a regular schedule of outstanding daytime shows, usually from Friday to Sunday, with occasional weekday performances.

✉ 14 Dagmar Passage, off Cross Street, Islington ☎ 020 7226 1787 Ⓣ Angel, Highbury, Islington 🖐 Moderate

London Duck Tours

London's most unusual river ride is aboard a yellow amphibious ex-World War II DUKW (Duck) vehicle, operated by London Duck Tours. The journey begins in conventional style on dry land, but just watch the kids' faces as their land vehicle suddenly splashes into the water for a 75-minute tour of the sights.

✉ Departs from Chicheley Street (behind the London Eye) ☎ 020 7928 3132 (reservations essential) 👋 Expensive

Museums and galleries

All the major museums and galleries have special projects for youngsters. At the British Museum (➤ 36–37), for example, drop by the Paul Hamlyn Library next to Room 2 and find out about the family trails and free Ford activity backpacks, full of puzzles, games and other activities to do in the galleries with the whole family.

Pollock's Toy Museum

For 40 years, this unusual museum has fascinated youngsters with its doll's houses and teddy bears, mechanical toys, magic lanterns and board games. The oldest toy? A 4,000-year-old Egyptian toy mouse.

✉ 1 Scala Street ☎ 020 7636 3452 👋 Inexpensive 🚇 Goodge Street

Best shopping areas

Bond Street

London's most exclusive shopping street is expensive for buying, but a great place for just looking. *Haute couture*, antiques, auction houses, fine-art galleries and jewellers predominate.

🚇 Green Park, Bond Street

Carnaby Street

After the heyday of the Swinging 60s, the boutiques in and around Carnaby Street are once again trendy, with hot and hip designers, such as Beyond the Valley (2 Newburgh Street), as well as retro designs from the past four decades.

🚇 Oxford Street, Piccadilly Circus

Covent Garden area

Covent Garden piazza and its boutiques are thronged with tourists as well as locals, so seek out the dozens of one-of-a-kind shops within 10 minutes' walk along Maiden Lane and Henrietta Street, Wellington Street and Floral Street, Neal Street and Long Acre. Tucked away is Neal's Yard, with its hippy feel.

🚇 Covent Garden

Kensington High Street/Church Street

Kensington High Street features all the major UK chain stores – and then some. By contrast, Kensington Church Street curves past art and antiques dealers, patisseries and wine shops.

🚇 Kensington High Street

King's Road

This area has had a renaissance. In a courtyard just off Sloane Square, Duke of York Square boasts fun shops and cafés. The further you walk down King's Road, the more unusual the shops.
🚇 Sloane Square

Oxford Street

With 300 stores, 2.5km (1.5-mile) long Oxford Street is Europe's busiest shopping street. At Oxford Circus, Topshop is iconic; towards Marble Arch are department stores such as John Lewis (No 300) and Selfridges (No 400) and Marks & Spencer (No 458).
🚇 Marble Arch, Bond Street, Oxford Circus, Tottenham Court Road

Piccadilly and more

Parallel to bustling Piccadilly, Jermyn Street's shops (► 79) have clothed and booted London's aristocrats for 350 years.
🚇 Piccadilly Circus, Green Park

Regent Street

A handsome boulevard with many exclusive shops including gold, silver and jewellery at Mappin & Webb and Garrard & Co; toys at Hamleys (► 68), and stylish clothes at Liberty (► 155).
🚇 Oxford Circus

Sloane Street/Knightsbridge

Armani, Chanel, Dior, Gucci, D&G, Hermès, Pucci, Yves Saint Laurent and Valentino are just some of the designer names to be found here. Explore Harrods (► 129) on the Brompton Road.
🚇 Sloane Square (south end), Knightsbridge (north end)

Westfield London

London's biggest mall with 265 designer and high street stores.
✉ West Cross Route, Shepherd's Bush ☎ 020 3371 2300;
http://uk.westfield.com/london 🚇 Wood Lane, Shepherd's Bush

Exploring

St James's, Mayfair and Piccadilly 75–92

The City and East 93–110

Westminster and the South Bank 111–126

Knightsbridge, Kensington and Chelsea 127–140

Covent Garden, Bloomsbury and Soho 141–156

Outer London 157–171

London is one of the world's few truly great cities. Its depth of history is unrivalled by any other major capital, its shopping is the envy of Europe, and it has been undergoing a renaissance in cuisine and fashion. With around 30 million visitors per year and one of the world's most cosmopolitan indigenous populations, it is a global melting pot, catering for all tastes and nationalities.

Of course, not all is perfect. Hotel prices are too high, the weather is unpredictable (so be prepared!) and the traffic can be horrendous. On the other hand, London is a very civilized city. Life may be fast and sometimes impersonal, but it is very rarely aggressive, and oases of calm – the parks, historic churches, museums, and hotels and department stores serving afternoon tea – are never more than a few steps away.

St James's, Mayfair and Piccadilly

If you only had one day in the city this area, between Buckingham Palace and Trafalgar Square, is full of highlights and gives an insight into traditional, quintessential London.

MAYFAIR

ST JAMES'S

This affluent area contains some of the city's grandest architecture, leafiest squares and prettiest parks, as well as exclusive shopping opportunities. Buckingham Palace, the Queen's official London residence, sits at the end of the grand, tree-lined processional Mall and is at the top of the list for many visitors, particularly for the famous Changing of the Guard ceremony. Not far away is the much older St James's Palace and adjacent is Clarence House, London home of Prince Charles and the Duchess of Cornwall.

For a fun night out, nowhere bustles more than Piccadilly Circus and Leicester Square, in the heart of London's Theatreland; Shaftesbury Avenue alone has six major theatres – quite a contrast

with Piccadilly's shops, the Royal Academy's paintings or the peace of St James's Park and Green Park. In Trafalgar Square – known worldwide for Nelson's Column – is the National Gallery, home to the country's premier art collection.

BANQUETING HOUSE

Banqueting House is the only
surviving part of the grand
Whitehall Palace, which
burned down in 1698.
Designed in classical style by
Inigo Jones, it was completed
in 1622 and is famous for its magnificent ceiling painting by
Rubens. This huge work was commissioned by Charles I to
celebrate the wisdom of the reign of the Stuart dynasty and
depicts his father, James I. It was therefore to provide an ironic
backdrop to the events of 30 January 1649 when Charles,
defeated in the English Civil War, stepped out from a window of

Banqueting House on to a scaffold to face the
executioner's axe. The vaulted undercroft
(crypt), formerly the wine cellar of James I,
is also open to the public.

www.hrp.org.uk

✚ 15H ✉ Whitehall ☎ 0844 482 7777
🕓 Mon–Sat 10–5. Closed 24 Dec–1 Jan, Good Fri,
all public hols and for functions at short notice
✋ Inexpensive 🍴 Café-in-the-Crypt, St. Martin-in-
the-Fields, Trafalgar Square (£; ➤ 58)
🚇 Westminster, Embankment

BUCKINGHAM PALACE

World famous as the London home of the Queen, this vast,
sprawling, 775-room house was built mostly between 1820 and
1837, although the familiar East Front public face of the palace was
not added until 1913. Visitors get to view the **State Rooms,** which
are furnished with some of the most important works of art from
the Royal Collection – one of the largest and most valuable private
art collections in the world. There's no chance of spotting any of
the royal family, however, as they are always away when the

palace is open. Around the corner, on Buckingham Palace Road, is the **Queen's Gallery**, with regularly changing themed exhibitions of treasures from the Royal Collection. Alongside, the **Royal Mews** are still working stables, with fine horses and grand vehicles, including the Gold State Coach. Save money and time with a combined ticket for all three.

Changing the Guard is still the most popular reason for visiting the palace. The ceremony takes place daily from May to July and on alternate days the rest of the year (weather permitting). At around 11:15 the St James's Palace part of the old guard marches down the Mall to meet the old guard of Buckingham Palace. There they await the arrival, at 11:30, of the new guard from Wellington Barracks, who are accompanied by a band. Keys are ceremonially handed from the old to the new guard while the band plays. When

the sentries have been changed, at around 12:05, the old guard returns to Wellington Barracks and the new part of the St James's Palace guard marches off to St James's Palace. As it can be extremely busy, aim to get close to the railings well before 11, particularly in high summer.

www.royal.gov.uk; **www**.royalcollection.org.uk

✚ 9E ✉ The Mall ☎ 020 7766 7300

State Rooms

✉ Buckingham Palace 🕘 Tours daily late Jul–Sep 9:45–3:45 (last tour) 👋 Very expensive 🚇 Green Park, Hyde Park Corner, St James's Park, Victoria ❓ Timed tickets from Ticket Office, Visitor Entrance, Buckingham Palace Road on day of visit or in advance by credit card ☎ 020 7766 7300

Queen's Gallery

✉ Buckingham Palace Road ☎ 020 7766 7301 🕘 Daily 10–5:30 (last admission 4:30) 👋 Moderate

Royal Mews

✉ Buckingham Palace Road ☎ 020 7766 7302 🕘 Late Mar–late Jul Sat–Thu 11–4 (last admission 3:15); late Jul–late Sep daily 10–5 (last admission 4:15); late Sep–late Oct Sat–Thu 11–4 (last admission 3:15) 👋 Expensive 🚇 Hyde Park Corner, St James's Park, Victoria, Green Park

CABINET WAR ROOMS AND CHURCHILL MUSEUM

This underground warren of rooms provided a secure home for the War Cabinet and their military advisers during World War II and was used by Sir Winston Churchill on over 100 occasions. Today it is a time capsule, with the clocks stopped at 4:58pm on 15 October 1940 and the ghost of Churchill hanging heavy in the air. You can view his private kitchen, dining room and his wife's bedroom. Many of his speeches were made from here and some are played to heighten the evocative atmosphere.

www.cwr.iwm.org.uk
✚ 11E ✉ Clive Steps, King Charles Street ☎ 020 7930 6961 🕐 Daily 9:30–6 (last admission 5). Closed 24–26 Dec
💷 Expensive (under 16 free)
🍴 Switchroom Café (£)
Ⓜ Westminster ❓ Admission includes audio guide

JERMYN STREET

With elegant, Dickensian-looking shops dating back to the 18th and 19th centuries, Jermyn Street is the essence of 'Gentleman's London'. Order handmade shoes at Tricker's (No 67) or a shirt at Hilditch & Key (Nos 73 and 37); taste traditional cheeses at Paxton & Whitfield (No 93).

www.jermynstreet.net
✚ 14H Ⓜ Green Park, Piccadilly Circus

NATIONAL GALLERY

Best places to see, ➤ 42–43.

NATIONAL PORTRAIT GALLERY

Founded in 1856 as a 'British Historical Portrait Gallery', the gallery's earliest contemporary portrait is that of Henry VII, from 1505.

If you want to see the exhibits in chronological order go up to the top floor and work your way down. The collection is too large to be displayed at one time so it changes periodically. The pictures least likely to change are the oldest, many of which are of great historical value. Those most likely to be rotated are the portraits of late 20th-century figures; the display of new additions tends to be dictated by current public interest.

Most visitors' favourites are the very earliest (top floor), the most recent, the Victorian and the early 20th century galleries. Predictably, there are many images of royalty, and at opposite ends of the gallery is a wonderful contrast of styles featuring the likenesses of Elizabeth I and, some 400 years later, the present British queen, Elizabeth II. The 'Coronation Portrait' of Elizabeth I is an acclaimed masterpiece, while much more controversial is the colour screenprint, in signature fashion by Andy Warhol, of the current monarch. This also underlines the point that the gallery holds more than just conventional paintings; sculptures, photography, sketches, silhouettes, caricatures and other methods of portraiture are all featured. Among contemporary portraits you'll find soccer star David Beckham, musician Sir Paul McCartney and actors Sir Ian McKellen and Catherine Zeta-Jones.

www.npg.org.uk

➕ 15J ✉ St Martin's Place, Orange Street ☎ 020 7306 0055 🕓 Daily 10–6 (Thu, Fri until 9). Closed 24–26 Dec 💷 Free (except special exhibitions)
🍴 Rooftop restaurant (££), café (£) 🚇 Leicester Square, Charing Cross
❓ Audio guides to over 170 portraits; frequent lectures and tours

PICCADILLY CIRCUS

This is a rendezvous for shoppers, theatregoers, clubbers and restaurant-goers. 'Circus' is an old-fashioned term for a road intersection; 'Piccadilly' refers to Pickadilly Hall, a 17th-century tailor's shop that sold 'pickadills', lace collars. The so-called statue of Eros actually represents the Angel of Christian Charity, a tribute to the philanthropic Lord Shaftesbury. London's virtual-reality adventure haven is the Trocadero and inside is **Ripley's Believe it or Not!** 'odditorium', which has 800 weird and wonderful exhibits.

➕ 14J 🚇 Piccadilly Circus

Ripley's Believe it or Not!

✉ 1 Piccadilly Circus ☎ 020 3238 0022 🕙 Daily 10–midnight 💷 Expensive

ROYAL ACADEMY OF ARTS

The RA is the country's oldest fine arts society and regularly stages world-class art exhibitions, most famously the annual Summer Exhibition (in June). The elegant home of the RA, Burlington House, features some fine 18th-century ceiling paintings and has opened its Fine Rooms to provide a permanent display space. This includes major works by leading British artists from Reynolds to Hockney, plus Britain's sole Michelangelo marble sculpture.

www.royalacademy.org.uk

🔲 13J ✉ Burlington House, Piccadilly ☎ 020 7300 8000. Advance tickets 0844 209 1919 🕓 Daily during exhibition 10–6 (Fri until 10). Fine Rooms Tue–Fri 1–4:30; Sat, Sun 10–6. Closed 25 Dec 🍴 Exhibitions moderate; Fine Rooms: free 🍴 Café (£), buffet restaurant (££) 🚇 Green Park, Piccadilly Circus

ST JAMES'S CHURCH

This 'little piece of heaven in Piccadilly' was built between 1676 and 1684 by Christopher Wren, though it was badly damaged in World War II and has been heavily restored. The main artistic interest of the church is the work of Grinling Gibbons, the greatest woodcarver in 17th-century England. However, the church's popularity, particularly with

local Londoners, lies in the numerous cultural activities it promotes, including an arts and crafts market, an antiques market and regular top-class concerts and recitals.

www.st-james-piccadilly.org

🔼 14J ✉ 197 Piccadilly ☎ 020 7734 4511 🕐 Daily 8–6:30 ✋ Free
🍴 Café (£) 🚇 Green Park, Piccadilly Circus ❓ Concerts, recitals: Mon, Wed, Fri at 1:10 (free).
Evening concerts usually Thu, Fri, Sat 7:30 (expensive). Craft market Wed–Sat 11–6; antiques market Tue 10–6

ST JAMES'S PALACE

After the Palace of Whitehall was destroyed in 1698, the court moved to St James's Palace, which remained the official royal London residence until 1837, when Queen Victoria decamped to Buckingham Palace. Now the palace is used for official receptions. To see inside the Chapel Royal or the Queen's Chapel (across the street), you can attend a Sunday morning service. Adjacent to the palace is **Clarence House,** formerly home to the late Queen Mother, but now occupied by the Prince of Wales. It is open to the public during the summer.

www.royal.gov.uk

🔼 10E ✉ Chapel Royal, St James's Palace 🕐 Open for Sun morning services only. Chapel Royal: Oct–Good Fri; Queen's Chapel: Easter Sun–Jul
✋ Free 🍴 Inn the Park (£–££; ➤ 58) 🚇 Green Park

Clarence House

☎ 020 7766 7303 🕐 Aug–late Sep daily 10–4 by pre-booked, timed guided tour only ✋ Moderate

ST JAMES'S PARK

The prettiest of central London's royal parks, St James's was established by Henry VIII in the 1530s. Don't miss the magical views from the bridge in the centre of the lake, west to Buckingham Palace and east to the domes and towers of Whitehall.

www.royalparks.org.uk

✚ 11E 👣 Free 🚇 St James's Park

ST JAMES'S STREET

St James's is 'Clubland' and here you will find four of its most distinguished 'gentlemen's clubs': White's (No 37–38), where Prince Charles held his stag party in 1981; Boodle's (No 28), haunt of London's chief 19th-century dandy, Beau Brummell; Brooks's (No 60), once renowned for its gambling; and the Carlton (No 69), bastion of

the Conservative party, whose male-only rules were bent for Mrs Thatcher when she was Prime Minister. Admission to all clubs is by membership only.

Of more general interest are three of London's most intriguing small shops. John Lobb's at No 9 was established in 1849 and has been 'bootmakers to the Crown' since 1863. Look inside the shop's small museum case for historical items such as the wooden last that was used for Queen Victoria's shoes. At No 6 is James Lock & Co, family-owned and run since 1676, which has provided headwear for national heroes such as Nelson and Wellington and where the bowler hat was invented. Established in 1698 and still family-run, wine merchants Berry Brothers & Rudd are at No 3, adjacent to a narrow alley leading to tiny Pickering Place where, between 1842 and 1845, the Republic of Texas kept a legation (diplomatic ministry). A plaque marks the spot.

🞦 13H 🚇 Green Park

SPENCER HOUSE

Built between 1756 and 1766 for Earl Spencer (an ancestor of the late Diana, Princess of Wales), Spencer House is London's finest surviving mid-18th century house. After being completely restored at a cost of £16 million, it was opened to visitors in 1990. The one-hour guided tour takes in eight rooms featuring elegant gilded decorations and period paintings and furniture.

www.spencerhouse.co.uk

🞦 13H ✉ 27 St James's Place ☎ 020 7499 8620 ⏰ Sun 10:30–5:45. Closed Jan, Aug. Access by 1-hour tour only 🖐 Moderate 🍴 Quaglino's (£££; ➤ 90) 🚇 Green Park 🛈 No children under 10

TRAFALGAR SQUARE

This is the geographical centre of London; all road distances are measured from here and at its heart is Nelson's Column. The buildings of South Africa House, Canada House and the National Gallery line three sides of the square, while the fourth opens to Whitehall. The square takes its name from the Battle of Trafalgar in 1805, during which Admiral Nelson, Britain's greatest naval hero, commanded his fleet to the famous victory against Franco-Spanish forces. Nelson was killed during the battle and the column, 51.5m (169ft) high, was erected between 1839 and 1843.

Topped by the elegant steeple copied worldwide, St Martin-in-the-Fields was designed by James Gibbs in 1726. The church is active for both worship and for 350 concerts a year. However, its crypt is renowned as a meeting place for visitors and locals alike. The new glass pavilion entrance on the north side of the church leads down to the revamped shop, the concert box office, the Brass Rubbing Centre and, under ancient arches, the vast Café in the Crypt (➤ 58).

www.smitf.org

➕ 15H

St Martin-in-the-Fields

✉ Trafalgar Square ☎ General enquiries 020 7766 1100; concert enquiries 020 7766 1100 🕐 Church: Mon–Sat 8–6:30, Sun 8–7:30. Crypt brass rubbing centre: Mon–Wed 10–7, Thu–Sat 10–9, Sun 11:30–6. Concerts: Mon, Tue, Fri at 1pm. Candlelit concerts of baroque music: most Tue, Thu–Sat 7:30 👋 Free. Lunchtime concerts donation, evening concerts expensive 🍴 Café in the Crypt (£; ➤ 58) 🚇 Charing Cross, Leicester Square

WHITEHALL

Whitehall has been the country's principal corridor of power since the early 18th century. The epicentre is Downing Street, home to the Prime Minister and to the Chancellor of the Exchequer, while north and south are various imposing buildings that house the country's top civil servants and ministries.

Just south of Downing Street is the Cenotaph, the national memorial to the dead of the two World Wars. The street was named after Henry VIII's Whitehall Palace, which burned down in 1698, leaving Banqueting House (➤ 76) as the sole surviving building above ground. Opposite here is Horse Guards, the official entrance to the royal palaces, still guarded by two mounted troopers and a good place to watch one of London's guard-changing ceremonies.

✚ 15H 🚫 No public access to Downing Street 🍴 Café in the Crypt (£; ➤ 58) 🚇 South end Westminster; north end Charing Cross ❓ Horse Guards guard changes Mon–Sat 11am, Sun 10am; ceremonial dismounting and inspection daily at 4. National Remembrance Service held at the Cenotaph at 11am on Sun nearest 11 Nov

HOTELS

Athenaeum (£££)

This elegant hotel overlooking Green Park remains one of the most popular and friendly in the area. Lovely bedrooms and a spa for the exclusive use of guests.

✉ Piccadilly ☎ 020 7499 3464; www.athenaeumhotel.com 🚇 Green Park

B&B Belgravia (££)

The smartest new B&B to open in London in recent years, the B&B Belgravia is also affordable. It is popular with leisure travellers and businessmen and a healthy breakfast is included in the price.

✉ 64–66 Ebury Street ☎ 020 7259 8570; www.bb-belgravia.com 🚇 Victoria

The Goring (£££)

Among London's most famous family-run hotels, providing a wonderful example of old-fashioned hospitality and service.

✉ Beeston Place, Grosvenor Gardens ☎ 020 7396 9000; www.thegoring.com 🚇 Victoria

Le Meridien Piccadilly (£££)

For many, this well-established luxury hotel lies at the very hub of London life. Bedrooms are finished to a high standard.

✉ 21 Piccadilly ☎ 020 7734 8000; www.lemeridien.com 🚇 Piccadilly Circus

Sanctuary House Hotel (££)

You can expect reasonably priced comfort within walking distance of Buckingham Palace, Westminster Abbey and the Houses of Parliament. Owned by Fuller's brewery, you can taste their award-winning beers in the ground floor Ale & Pie House.

✉ 33 Tothill Street ☎ 020 7799 4044; www.fullershotels.com
🚇 St James's Park

The Stafford (£££)

Tucked away in exclusive St James's, offering the height of luxury. Elegant, individually designed bedrooms and beautiful public areas.

✉ 16–18 St James's Place ☎ 020 7493 0111; www.the staffordhotel.co.uk
🚇 Green Park

Trafalgar (££)

Just off Trafalgar Square, this was the first of Hilton's leading-edge hip hotels. Think art and music, young and trendy, with a glorious rooftop terrace. Nothing like the usual Hilton.

✉ 2 Spring Gardens ☎ 020 7870 2900; www.thetrafalgar.com 🚇 Charing Cross, Embankment.

The Washington Mayfair Hotel (£££)

A stylish but affordable favourite for the past 100 years, this is within easy reach of Mayfair's attractions. Own restaurant, popular cocktail bar and gymnasium.

✉ 5 Curzon Street ☎ 020 7499 7000; www.washington-mayfair.co.uk 🚇 Bond Street, Oxford Circus, Piccadilly Circus, Green Park

The Westbury (£££)

Refurbishment has brought back the chic to a hotel steps away from the glamour of Bond Street, Regent Street and Piccadilly.

✉ 37 Conduit Street ☎ 020 7629 7755; www.westburymayfair.com 🚇 Bond Street, Oxford Circus, Piccadilly Circus, Green Park

RESTAURANTS

Al Duca (£–££)

The nearest to a neighbourhood restaurant in posh St James's, the informal Al Duca features modern Italian dishes: imaginative pasta combinations, grilled meats and vegetables. Italian wine list.

✉ 4–5 Duke of York Street ☎ 020 7839 3090 ⊙ Mon–Sat lunch, dinner 🚇 Piccadilly Circus

Café in the Crypt (£)

See page 58.

Le Caprice (££–£££)

It may be famous as the place where celebrities eat, but mere mortals also receive star treatment, and the food is excellent. Modern European cuisine in a setting of timeless classic décor.

✉ Arlington House, Arlington Street ☎ 020 7629 2239 ⊙ Daily lunch, dinner 🚇 Green Park

Galileo's (£)

With non-stop service, this is useful for pre- and post-theatre dining. Stop for tea, coffee and freshly prepared Tuscan dishes.

✉ 71 Haymarket ☎ 020 7839 3939 🕐 Daily noon–11pm, Fri, Sat noon–11:30pm, Sun 12–10:30pm 🚇 Piccadilly Circus

Quaglino's (££–£££)

The dining room here seats 267 and resembles an ocean liner but there's nearly always a real buzz to this theatrical restaurant. Modern European cuisine in a very French bistro/brasserie atmosphere.

✉ 16 Bury Street ☎ 020 7930 6767 🕐 Mon–Sat lunch, dinner 🚇 Green Park

Rasa W1 (£–££)

This restaurant's simple dining rooms on two floors feature marble floor tiles and a spiral staircase between the two. The highly acclaimed vegetarian menu comes from Kerala in southern India, though meat-eaters are also accommodated.

✉ 6 Dering Street ☎ 020 7629 1346 🕐 Mon–Sat lunch, dinner daily 🚇 Bond Street, Oxford Circus

Truc Vert (£)

A café, restaurant and deli all in one, this slice of rustic France provides breakfast lunch and dinner for all budgets close to Oxford Street shopping. But you can also order an English-style afternoon tea!

✉ 42 North Audley Street ☎ 020 7491 9988 🕐 Mon–Fri 7:30am–10pm, Sat 9am–10pm, Sun 9–5 🚇 Marble Arch, Bond Street

The Wolseley (£–££)

The fashionable Wolseley is housed in an opulent art deco building. First-class Modern British café-style food is served throughout the day, perfect for breakfast or afternoon tea. There is also a shop selling smart tableware, teas and coffees.

✉ 160 Piccadilly ☎ 020 7499 6996 🕐 Mon–Fri 7am–midnight, Sat 8am–midnight, Sun 8am–6:30pm 🚇 Green Park

SHOPPING

BEAUTY AND COSMETICS

DR Harris
After 200 years, regulars still buy tried and trusted skin care products, such as almond hand wash, milk cucumber and roses lotion, as well as English lavender soaps and men's shaving products.

✉ 29 St James's Street ☎ 020 7930 3915 Ⓜ Green Park, Piccadilly Circus

Molton Brown
A seductive aroma greets you as you cross the threshold. Shampoos, bath oils and scented candles that are hard to resist.

✉ 58 South Molton Street ☎ 020 7499 6474 Ⓜ Bond Street

CLOTHING AND ACCESSORIES

Browns
One of London's best designer boutiques, claiming to hold the biggest range of labels. For discount gear try their branch Browns Labels for Less, just a few steps away at 50 South Molton Street.

✉ 23–27 South Molton Street ☎ 020 7514 0000 Ⓜ Bond Street, Green Park

Burberry
The famous Burberry check is not just confined to trenchcoats and scarves. Choose from over 300 lines at this very British institution.

✉ 21–23 New Bond Street ☎ 020 7968 0000 Ⓜ Bond Street, Green Park

Fenwick
For decades this has been one of London's most stylish stores, with its wide range of designers for women, though it also has menswear. Great accessories.

✉ 63 New Bond Street ☎ 020 7629 9161 Ⓜ Bond Street, Oxford Circus

Dover Street Market
One of London's most exciting shopping spaces: six minimalist floors of sharp fashion, including the full range of Comme des Garçons designs.

✉ 17–18 Dover Street ☎ 020 7518 0680 Ⓜ Green Park

FOOD AND DRINK
Fortnum & Mason
Predating the supermarket, the Fortnum & Mason's Food Hall has been supplying the nobility with hampers since the days of Queen Victoria and is the main attraction at this classy department store. It is particularly well known for its tea, coffee and chocolate selections.

✉ 181 Piccadilly ☎ 020 7734 8040 Ⓔ Piccadilly Circus, Green Park

MUSIC
Chappell of Bond Street
Relocated to a store in Soho, Chappell has the largest selection of classical and popular sheet music in Europe. Also keyboards, brass and woodwind instruments.

✉ 152–160 Wardour Street ☎ 020 7432 4400 Ⓔ Oxford Circus, Tottenham Court Road

ENTERTAINMENT

The West End is the largest theatre district in the world, with some 50 venues attracting 13 million customers every year. The Society of London Theatre, the official association for the London theatre industry (www.solt.co.uk), runs **tkts**, formerly the 'Half Price Ticket Booth', on the south side of Leicester Square. It offers half-price and discounted tickets, usually for about 30 shows each day. Stand in line for shows on the day or even as far as seven days ahead (www.tkts.co.uk; open Mon–Sat 10–7, Sun 12–3).

MUSIC
London Coliseum
Home of the English National Opera – which performs only in English. The English National Ballet performs here at Christmas.

✉ St Martin's Lane ☎ 020 7632 8300 Ⓔ Charing Cross, Leicester Square

Dover Street
London's biggest live music restaurant, seating some 400 people, where the musical menu is jazz, blues, soul and R'n'B.

✉ 8–10 Dover Street ☎ 020 7629 9813 Ⓔ Green Park, Piccadilly Circus

The City and East

The City of London, the heart and financial centre of the old capital, is one of the busiest commercial hubs in the world, with banks, corporate headquarters and insurance companies occupying dramatic showcases of modern architecture. Yet alongside these, you'll find hidden 17th-century churches, cobbled alleyways, historic markets and fragments of the original Roman city wall.

ST LUKE'S

HOLBORN

CITY

Much of the medieval city was destroyed in the Great Fire of 1666, and in the construction that followed as many as 50 Wren churches were built, including St Paul's Cathedral. Three of

London's most iconic sights – St Paul's, the Tower of London and London Bridge – are in this district. The City of London is home to the modern Barbican Centre, a performing arts venue, and to the Museum of London, where the story of the capital is brought to life. To the west are four historic Inns of Court, the heart of legal London. Stretching downstream to the east lies Docklands, a huge area of urban redevelopment. Here is a vibrant, diverse and culturally interesting area with historic warehouses, riverside pubs and restaurants.

BANK OF ENGLAND MUSEUM

The story of Britain's monetary and banking system since 1694 is told at this museum. The Bank of England is the nation's central bank, functioning at the heart of one of the world's largest and most sophisicated financial centres. A visit to this small but lively museum will enlighten you as to its workings and its history. Having been in existence so long, the bank has accumulated a considerable number of items associated with its history. The collections include banknotes and coins, furniture, books, pictures and statues. Highlights are its real gold bullion (each house-brick-sized bar is worth around £70,000), the reproduction banking hall and the award-winning interactive screens and currency dealing computer game.

www.bankofengland.co.uk/museum

✚ 21K ✉ Bartholomew Lane ☎ 020 7601 5545 🕓 Mon–Fri 10–5 👆 Free ⑪ The Don (£–££, ➤ 108) Ⓔ Bank

THE CHARLES DICKENS MUSEUM

Dating from 1801, this elegant residence is the only surviving house in which Charles Dickens lived for any length of time while in London. He stayed here from April 1837 to December 1839, long enough to secure his burgeoning reputation by writing the final instalments of *The Pickwick Papers*, almost all of *Oliver Twist*, the whole of *Nicholas Nickleby* and the start of *Barnaby Rudge*. Opened as a museum in 1925, the house now holds the finest collection of Dickens memorabilia in existence, with many of the exhibits reflecting the novels that were written here.

www.dickensmuseum.com

✚ 17M ✉ 48 Doughty Street ☎ 020 7405 2127

🕐 Mon–Sat 10–5, Sun 11–5 (last admission 4:30) ✋ Inexpensive 🍴 The Lamb (£–££; ➤ 66) Ⓜ Russell Square, Chancery Lane

COURTAULD GALLERY

The Courtauld Gallery displays some of the most familiar paintings in the world, mainly from the high-quality collection amassed by industrialist Samuel Courtauld in the 1920s. And all are housed in the impressive Somerset House, a grand 18th-century palace overlooking the River Thames.

The Impressionists and Post-Impressionists are top priority, particularly Van Gogh's *Self Portrait with Bandaged Ear* and Manet's *A Bar at the Folies Bergère*. Other paintings include a version of *Le Déjeuner sur l'Herbe*, also by Manet, *The Card Players* by Cézanne, *La Loge* by Renoir, *Two Dancers on a Stage* by Degas and Gauguin's Tahitian works. The collection goes back to the 14th century, and early masterpieces include works by Cranach the Elder, a superb Holy Trinity by Botticelli and from the early 17th century a large number of paintings by Rubens. There are also some fine 20th-century works, including Matisse.

www.courtauld.ac.uk/gallery

✚ 17J ✉ Somerset House, Strand ☎ 020 7848 2526 🕐 Daily 10–6 (last admission 5:30) ✋ Inexpensive; children free. Free Mon 10–2 (except public hols) 🍴 Gallery Café (£) Ⓜ Temple (closed Sun), Covent Garden, Holborn

DOCKLANDS

London's Docklands stretch some 8km
(5 miles) east of the Tower of London to
the old Royal Docks. Historically, this area
was the powerhouse of the Empire, at its
height the busiest port in the world. It
reached the peak of its activity in 1964 but
changes in technology (most notably
containerization) signalled its demise.
Within a decade most of the quays and
great swathes of nearby land were derelict
and remained so until the 1980s when the
government began the world's largest
urban redevelopment project to date. For
an excellent insight into the area's rich
history visit the Museum of London
Docklands, West India Quay (daily 10–6).

The centrepiece is One Canada Square,
Britain's tallest building at 243m (797ft).
A trip on the Docklands Light Railway is
recommended for its high-level views into this Brave New London
World. The latest DLR line, to London City Airport, opened in 2005.
Try also the area's historical riverside pubs, which include the
Prospect of Whitby, the Mayflower and the Grapes.
www.dockland.co.uk
✚ 24H (off map)

FLEET STREET

Fleet Street became the original publishing centre of London in
1500, when England's first press was set up here. From 1702 until
the 1980s it was also the home of England's newspapers until
new technology meant they could decamp to cheaper, more
efficient offices away from the 'Street of Ink'. Today it is still worth
a visit for St Bride's Church (▶ 104) and, just north of here, Wine

Office Court, home to Ye Olde Cheshire Cheese pub, while close by is **Dr Johnson's House,** built around 1700 and now a museum dedicated to the writer who gave us the first English-language dictionary.

Dr Johnson's House

🚹 18K ✉ 17 Gough Square ☎ 020 7353 3745; www.drjohnsonshouse.org 🕐 Mon–Sat 11–5:30, (Oct–Apr 11–5) 💷 Moderate 🍴 Ye Olde Cheshire Cheese (£; ➤ 109) Ⓜ Chancery Lane, Temple, Holborn

GUILDHALL

The City of London has been governed from this site for over 800 years and the majestic centrepiece of the Great Hall dates back to 1430. Its huge crypt is older, dating from the mid-13th century, and even older are the excavated remains of London's only Roman amphitheatre. The banners and stained-glass coats of arms that

decorate the hall belong to the City Livery companies, formed in medieval times to represent and support their professions, and still in existence today. Within the complex is the world's oldest Clock Museum and the Guildhall Art Gallery.

www.cityoflondon.gov.uk

🚹 21K ✉ Guildhall, Gresham Street ☎ 020 7606 3030 🕐 Great Hall and amphitheatre Mon–Sat 10–5. Closed for ceremonies and events. Art Gallery: Mon–Sat 10–5, Sun 12–4. Clock Museum: Mon–Sat 9:30–4:45 ☎ 020 7332 1868 💷 Great Hall, amphitheatre, Clock Museum free; art gallery inexpensive (free all day Fri and after 3:30 on other days) 🍴 The Place Below (£), St Mary-le-Bow Church, Cheapside Ⓜ Bank, St Paul's, Mansion House

INNS OF COURT

The Inns of Court, the training grounds for the country's barristers (lawyers), date from medieval times. Today only four survive: Inner Temple, Middle Temple, Lincoln's Inn and Gray's Inn. Each resembles a small college campus, with a library, chapel, hall and barristers' chambers (offices). Their grounds, usually open Monday to Friday, are central London's most charming and peaceful oases, and their narrow alleyways and small courtyards, many still gaslit, are very atmospheric in the early evening (➤ 100–101).

✚ 18K 👟 Free 🚇 Temple, Holborn, Chancery Lane

LLOYD'S BUILDING

Designed by Richard Rogers, of Georges Pompidou Centre (Paris) fame, this stunning glass and steel tower ('a post-modern oil refinery' said one critic) was the most controversial building in England when finished in 1986. It is closed to the public but remains one of London's most potent architectural statements.

✚ 22K ✉ One Lime Street ⏱ Closed to public 🍴 Leadenhall Wine & Tapas Bar (£), Leadenhall Market 🚇 Aldgate, Liverpool Street

MONUMENT

The Monument was erected to commemorate the Great Fire of London in 1666. Its height, 61m (200ft), is the exact distance to the bakery in Pudding Lane, where the Great Fire started. It was commissioned by King Charles II and designed by Christopher Wren and Robert Hooke. You can climb inside the column via a 311-step spiral staircase.

www.themonument.info

✚ 22J ✉ Monument Street ☎ 020 7626 2717 ⏱ Daily 9:30–5:30 👟 Inexpensive 🍴 Leadenhall Wine & Tapas Bar (£), Leadenhall Market 🚇 Monument

a walk around the Inns of Court

This walk should be done on a weekday as some areas within the Inns are closed at weekends.

Turn left out of Temple underground station, go up steps, turn right into Temple Place, then left on Milford Lane, then right through gate. Cross the car park, turn left through another gate; go up steps to Garden Court.

On your right are Middle Temple Gardens.

In Fountain Court, turn right.

On the right, Middle Temple Hall hosted the first performance of Shakespeare's *Twelfth Night* in 1602.

Continue under the arch to Lamb Building; walk up steps, bear left.

Ahead is Temple Church (1185), with its 13th-century Crusader knight effigies.

Leave Temple past Dr Johnson's Buildings, under the arch to Fleet Street.

On your right and up a flight of stairs is 400-year-old Prince Henry's Room and Pepys Exhibition (open Mon–Sat 11–2).

Cross Fleet Street, turn left, then right on Bell Yard, passing the Royal Courts of Justice. Turn left on Carey Street, right into New Square and Lincoln's Inn.

On your left is Lincoln's Inn hall; to the right the 1623 chapel.

Continue through Old Square, turn right at Stone Buildings; exit through a gate to Chancery Lane. Turn right, then left into Southampton Buildings.

On your left are the Silver Vaults, 30 shops selling a huge range of antique silver.

At the end of Southampton Buildings, enter Staple Inn, turn left for High Holborn. Cross High Holborn, turn left, then right into Gray's Inn, by the Cittie of York pub. Turn left into Field Court, past Gray's Inn Gardens. To the left, Fulwood Place leads back to High Holborn and Chancery Lane Tube station.

Distance Approximately 4km (2.5 miles)
Time 2–3 hours depending on visits
Start point 🚇 Temple (closed Sun) ✚ 17J
End point 🚇 Chancery Lane (closed Sun) ✚ 18L
Lunch Cittie of York, Holborn (£)

MUSEUM OF LONDON

Perhaps the most comprehensive city museum in the world, the multi-award-winning Museum of London presents a lively account of well over 2,000 years of history, reflecting the way people lived as much as buildings that have been excavated. The latest permanent exhibit, all about London and Londoners from 1666 to the present day, is fascinating for all the family.

Displays are chronological, starting with the prehistory gallery that follows the story of Londoners before Roman settlement, progressing to Roman London. The latter is a highlight, with reconstructed rooms and superb sculptures from the Temple of

Mithras discovered close by. The Medieval gallery shows objects from recent excavations, never displayed before, shedding light on the Dark Ages of the 15th century and going through more enlightened times up to 1558. Highlights include an audiovisual on the Black Death, a reconstruction of an Anglo-Saxon home and objects from 13th-century Jewish houses in the City of London. In the Stuart section you will find Oliver Cromwell's death mask, the Cheapside (jewellery) Hoard, plague exhibits and the Great Fire Experience, accompanied by a reading from the diary of Samuel Pepys.

Further galleries, from late Stuart times to the present, feature many fascinating large-scale exhibits. Most handsome of all is the opulent Lord Mayor's State Coach, made in 1757. The World City galleries cover the period from the French Revolution to the outbreak of World War I, and in the Victorian Walk section are some fascinating reconstructions of London shop fronts.

www.museumoflondon.org.uk

🕂 20L ✉ London Wall ☎ 020 7001 9844 🕐 Daily 10–6
✋ Free 🍴 Good café-restaurant (£) 🚇 Barbican, St Paul's, Moorgate
❓ Family events, including costumed actors, most Sats, Suns and during school hols

ST BARTHOLOMEW THE GREAT

Founded in 1123 by Rahere, the court jester to Henry I, this is London's oldest church. The entrance is a half-timbered Tudor gatehouse, and the atmospheric interior is reminiscent of a small cathedral. It has the best Norman chancel in London (rivalled only by the Chapel of St John in the Tower of London, ➤ 51) with Norman piers supporting an upper gallery. Among the fine tomb monuments is that of Rahere, the church's founder.

www.greatstbarts.com

🕂 19L ✉ West Smithfield ☎ 020 7606 5171 🕐 Tue–Fri 8:30–5 (4 in winter), Sat 10:30–4, Sun 8:30–8 ✋ Inexpensive 🍴 Le Comptoir Gascon (£–££; ➤ 108) 🚇 Barbican, St Paul's, Farringdon

ST BRIDE'S CHURCH

England's first moveable type printing press operated alongside
St Bride's, starting a 500-year link with Fleet Street's newspaper
industry. The present church, completed in 1675, is by Christopher
Wren, though its interior is modern, having been gutted by a bomb
in 1940. The crypt holds an interesting small museum tracing the
history of the church and its long connection
with the Fleet Street newspaper trade.
www.stbrides.com

🖪 19K ✉ Fleet Street ☎ 020 7427 0133 🕙 Mon–Fri
8–6, Sat 11–3, Sun 10–1, 5–7:30 ✋ Free 🍴 Ye Olde
Cheshire Cheese (£; ➤ 109) 🚇 Blackfriars
❓ Lunchtime concerts (most of year, not Lent and Dec)
Tue, Fri 1:15, choral services Sun 11, 6:30

ST KATHARINE DOCKS

To experience London's huge dockland
warehouses as they used to be without
making the journey east, visit St Katharine
Docks (walk, ➤ 62–63), conveniently close to

the Tower of London. Here exotic items such as ostrich feathers, spices, teas and ivory (up to 22,000 tusks in a year) were once stored. The docks closed in 1968 and were developed to cater to the tourist trade with shops, restaurants and historic sailing ships at anchor. The picturesque late 18th-century Dickens Inn pub-restaurant has 17th-century timbers in its galleried frontage.
www.skdocks.co.uk

✚ 24H 🖐 Free 🍴 Dickens Inn (£) 🚇 Tower Hill

ST PAUL'S CATHEDRAL
Best places to see, ➤ 46–47.

ST STEPHEN WALBROOK
This is arguably the finest of all the City's churches. Built by Christopher Wren between 1672 and 1679, its dome was the first in England and was clearly a prototype for Wren's engineering *tour de force*, the dome of St Paul's Cathedral. The church was beautifully restored between 1978 and

1987, with the original dark-wood fittings making a striking contrast to the gleaming white marble floor and the controversial giant white 'Camembert cheese' stone altarpiece, designed by Sir Henry Moore in 1972.
www.ststephenwalbrook.net

✚ 21K ✉ 39 Walbrook ☎ 020 7283 4444 🕐 Mon–Thu 10–4, Fri 10–3 🖐 Free 🍴 Sweetings (££), 39 Queen Victoria Street 🚇 Bank, Cannon Street

SIR JOHN SOANE'S MUSEUM

In terms of size and layout, this extraordinary labyrinthine museum is the most unusual art and antiquities collection in the capital. It was formerly the home of the designer and architect Sir John Soane (1753–1837) and has, according to the terms specified by Soane himself, been kept exactly in its original condition. Much of this magpie collection is arranged around a central court and is aided and abetted by false walls, alcoves, domes and skylights. Its treasures include masterpieces (cleverly hung on hinged panels which go flat to the wall to save space) by Turner, Canaletto and Hogarth (including the famous *Rake's Progress* series), a sarcophagus from the Valley of the Kings, a bizarre Gothic folly entitled the 'Monk's Parlour', plus sculptures and stone fragments galore.

www.soane.org

🕂 17L 🖂 13 Lincoln's Inn Fields ☎ 020 7405 2107 🕔 Tue–Sat 10–5. Also first Tue of month 6–9. Closed all public hols 👑 Free (charge for exhibitions) 🍴 Lamb (➤ 66) 🚇 Holborn ❓ Excellent guided tour Sat 11 (inexpensive)

TOWER BRIDGE

One of London's best-known landmarks, Tower Bridge was built between 1886 and 1894 and hailed as one of the greatest engineering feats of its day. It is basically a classic Victorian iron and steel structure, clad in stone to match the medieval appearance of its neighbour, the Tower of London. Until quite recently it was the last road bridge across the Thames before the river reaches the North Sea, and it remains London's only drawbridge. This function was to allow large ships to pass into the busy Upper Pool of London, which was a hive of warehouse activity in Victorian times. At its peak, its bascules (drawbridges) were like yo-yos, up and down 50 times a day. Today they open on average around 18 times a week to allow tall ships, cruise ships and naval vessels through.

The structure now houses the **Tower Bridge Exhibition,** an informative multimedia exhibition that explains the history of the bridge. You can also step right into the bowels of the building to see the original Victorian engine rooms which were used to raise the bascules from 1894 to 1976. The high-level walkways, 43m (141ft) above the river, were designed to allow pedestrians to cross when the drawbridges were raised, and the views are unbeatable. Even from ground level Tower Bridge is one of the city's great vantage points.

www.towerbridge.org.uk

✚ 24H

Tower Bridge Exhibition

✉ Tower Bridge ☎ 020 7403 3761 🕓 Apr–Sep daily 10–6:30; Oct–Mar 9:30–6. Last admission 1 hour before closing 🖐 Moderate 🍴 Butler's Wharf Chop House (££; ➤ 58) 🚇 Tower Hill, London Bridge ❓ Bridge lift information line 020 7940 3984 or see website

TOWER OF LONDON

Best places to see, ➤ 50–51.

HOTELS

Citadines London Holborn–Covent Garden (££)
Within walking distance of many attractions, this is a practical modern hotel. The apartment-style rooms have kitchen facilities.
✉ 94–99 High Holborn ☎ 020 7395 8800; www.citadines.com
🚇 Holborn

The Hoxton (£)
Calling itself an 'urban lodge', the Hoxton has taken London by storm, offering stylish rooms at affordable prices. Like a low-cost airline, the earlier you book, the cheaper the price.
✉ 81 Great Eastern Street ☎ 020 7550 1000; www.hoxtonhotels.com
🚇 Old Street

The Tower (££)
Large, busy, modern hotel next to the Tower of London with views of Tower Bridge and St Katharine Docks.
✉ St Katharine's Way ☎ 0871 376 9036; www.guoman.com 🚇 Tower Hill

Travelodge (£)
Located in a quiet spot not far from Liverpool Street station; adequate rooms at a good rate. Ideal for families.
✉ 1 Harrow Place ☎ 0871 984 6190; www.travelodge.co.uk
🚇 Liverpool Street

RESTAURANTS AND PUBS

Le Comptoir Gascon (£–££)
Little sister of the expensive Club Gascon, this is authentic Southwestern France in London: cassoulet and duck confit, excellent desserts and wines.
✉ 63 Charterhouse Street ☎ 020 7608 0851 🚇 Farringdon

The Don (£–££)
In what were port cellars, this smart bistro scores for atmosphere as well as hearty portions of steak, terrine, duck and a really top-class wine list.
✉ 20 St Swithin's Lane ☎ 020 7626 2606 🚇 Bank

The Eagle (£–££)

An award-winning crowd-puller, popular with media types. Serves probably the best pub food in the whole of London: options may include marinaded rump steak or king prawn bruschetta.

✉ 159 Farringdon Road ☎ 020 7837 1353 🕐 Mon–Sat 12–11, Sun 12–5 🚇 Farringdon

Grazing (£)

Enthusiastic, above-average budget eatery near the Tower of London preparing British produce (bacon, beef, haggis) for breakfast and lunch (till 4pm).

✉ 19–21 Great Tower Street ☎ 020 7283 2932 🚇 Tower Hill, Monument

Great Eastern Dining Room (£–££)

Modern Japanese, Chinese and Singapore cooking rubs shoulders comfortably and successfully in this trendy Shoreditch restaurant, where you can order à la carte, although dishes are designed so they can be shared as part of a banquet.

✉ 54–56 Great Eastern Street ☎ 020 7613 4545 🚇 Old Street, Liverpool Street

The Lamb (£)

See page 66.

Prospect of Whitby (£)

This historic but touristy river pub is crammed with maritime paraphernalia. It was built in 1520 and was patronized by Dickens, Turner and Whistler.

✉ 57 Wapping Wall ☎ 020 7481 1095 🕐 Daily 🚇 Wapping

Ye Olde Cheshire Cheese (£)

Essentially unchanged since 1667, the Cheshire Cheese is one of London's oldest and certainly most atmospheric pubs. Try their famous steak and kidney pudding.

✉ Wine Office Court, 145 Fleet Street ☎ 020 7353 6170 🕐 Closed Sun evening 🚇 Chancery Lane, Temple

SHOPPING

MARKETS
Brick Lane and more

Alongside the mainly Bangladeshi shops and restaurants, an old brewery has been converted into buzzing weekend market. The Backyard has 100 stalls of jewellery, clothing, accessories, art and crafts (Sat 11–6, Sun 10–5); the Sunday UpMarket has 140 stalls selling fashion, accessories, crafts and more (Sun 10–5).

✉ Brick Lane 🕔 Daily 🚇 Aldgate East, Liverpool Street

Petticoat Lane

London's best-known Sunday market is actually held on Wentworth Street, between Middlesex Street and Goulston Street. Most of the 1,000 stalls sell clothing and leather goods.

✉ Wentworth Street 🕔 Mon–Fri 10–4:30, Sun 9–2 🚇 Aldgate

ENTERTAINMENT

MUSIC
Barbican

The London Symphony Orchestra (LSO) and English Chamber Orchestra are both resident at the Barbican.

✉ Silk Street ☎ 020 7638 8891 🚇 Barbican

The O_2 Arena

The former Millennium Dome is now the world's number one venue for rock concerts and sports events. At the British Music Experience, also beneath the dome, you can dance, play guitar and explore a museum dedicated to 60 years of British popular music.

✉ O_2 Arena, Greenwich ☎ 0844 856 0202; www.theo2.co.uk 🚇 North Greenwich

THEATRE
The Royal Shakespeare Company

Known as the RSC, this prestigious company is based at Stratford-upon-Avon in the English Midlands. With no permanent theatre in London, they do perform in London from time to time.

www.rsc.org.uk

Westminster and the South Bank

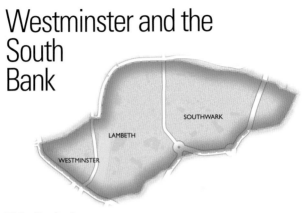

SOUTHWARK

LAMBETH

WESTMINSTER

This district is dominated by the Thames, an iconic symbol of the city. The river's banks present two contrasting images.

The north bank is lined, in general, with stately buildings connected with money, power and government and includes the

Houses of Parliament and Westminster Abbey. Here are buildings of political, historical and religious significance bringing a sense of stability to the city. Across the river, the South Bank has a very different flavour. Early theatre thrived here and Shakespeare's reconstructed Globe Theatre is testament to this. After World War II this area of wasteland was given a makeover with the construction of the Royal Festival Hall and the Southbank Centre. To celebrate the Millennium, innovative attractions opened that are still major international draws. The revolving London Eye was intended as a temporary structure, like the Eiffel Tower; and Tate Modern, the stunning conversion of an old power station, is now the world's most popular modern art museum.

BOROUGH MARKET

Fresh produce has been sold here for well over 700
years, but, in parallel with London's renaissance as a
foodie city, London's oldest market has also enjoyed
a dramatic rebirth. Join crowds tasting and sipping
their way round 150 or so stalls crammed beneath
railway arches. See the best British organic meats
and cheeses, fresh fish and seafood, European
delicacies, home-baked breads and cakes. Snack on
samples or join the line for the grilled chorizo rolls at
Brindisa, known for its Spanish produce; scoff cakes
from Konditor & Cook; buy 'the world's best fudge'
at Burnt Sugar, made from Fairtrade, unrefined sugar.
www.boroughmarket.org.uk

🚩 21H ✉ Southwark Street ☎ 020 7407 1002 🕐 Thu
11–5, Fri 12–6, Sat 9–4 🚇 London Bridge

CLINK PRISON MUSEUM

From the early 16th century until 1780, the Clink, 'a very dismal
hole', was the jail of the Bishops of Winchester, used to
incarcerate the lowlife of Bankside – including prostitutes, drunks,
debtors, and actors who had 'broken the peace'. In fact it was so
notorious that it entered the English language as a synonym for
jail. Not that the bishop held the moral high ground. He acted
effectively as protection racketeer and pimp, licensing, and
profiting from, the various illegal activities that went on in the
badlands of Bankside. You can learn all about these times at the
Clink Prison Museum. Alongside, part of a wall with a great rose
window is all that survives of the Bishop's Palace, Winchester
House, built in 1109.
www.clink.co.uk

🚩 21H ✉ 1 Clink Street ☎ 020 7403 0900 🕐 Mon–Fri 10–6, Sat, Sun 10–9
🚶 Inexpensive 🍴 fish!, Cathedral Street, Borough Market (££) 🚇 London
Bridge (10-min walk)

DESIGN MUSEUM

This was set up in 1989 as the brainchild of Britain's leading design and style guru, Sir Terence Conran, to promote an awareness of the importance of design and the contribution it makes to everyday life. In a hip conversion of a banana warehouse, see objects that are both familiar and puzzling, weird and wonderful masterpieces from architecture to car design, fashion to furniture, bicycles to laptops, it is well worth a visit. The collection divides broadly into two parts. The more conventional historic part shows the design evolution of familiar workaday items, such as domestic appliances, cameras and cars. The Contemporary Design Gallery is an intriguing showcase for the very latest ideas; some currently in production, some at prototype stage, others stuck permanently on the drawing board. Interactive computer stations cater to a new generation of would-be designers. There's a good shop and the stylish Design Museum Café.

www.designmuseum.org

➕ 24G ✉ 28 Shad Thames ☎ 0870 833 9955 🕐 Daily 10–5:45. Closed 25–26 Dec (last admission 5:15) 👆 Expensive 🍴 Café (£) 🚇 London Bridge, Tower Hill

HMS *BELFAST*

HMS *Belfast* is Europe's last surviving big warship from World War II and occupies a spectacular permanent mooring site on the Thames just upstream from Tower Bridge. Launched in 1938, she saw action in the Arctic, at the D-Day Normandy landings and in the Korean War from 1950 to 1952. Today her seven decks, which once accommodated a crew of up to 800 men, serve as a museum, giving landlubbers a salty flavour of the rigours of serving at sea. The bridge, galley, operations room, punishment cells, engine and boiler rooms can all be explored. There are also various naval displays. Check out the exhibition Life at Sea.

www.iwm.org.uk

✚ 22H ✉ Morgan's Lane, off Tooley Street ☎ 020 7940 6300 🕓 Mar–Oct daily 10–6; Nov–Feb 10–5. Closed 24–26 Dec (last admission 1 hour before closing) 👤 Expensive; children free 🍴 Café (£) Ⓔ London Bridge, Tower Hill. Ferry from Tower Millennium Pier to London Bridge City Pier in summer

HOUSES OF PARLIAMENT

Best places to see, ➤ 40–41.

IMPERIAL WAR MUSEUM

Dedicated to an account of world conflict during the 20th century, the Imperial War Museum has the most impressive entrance of any London museum. Suspended from the ceiling of its glass atrium and occupying two floors around the atrium are World War II fighter planes, biplanes from the Great War, a V2 rocket, a Polaris

missile, field guns, tanks, submarines, plus over 40 other large exhibits. This is a thought-provoking museum, telling the story of war dispassionately, often from the point of view of the ordinary soldier or the folks left at home. The emphasis is on the two World Wars. Each has a large walk-in section where you can experience the horrors of the trenches or the claustrophobia of an air-raid shelter, then the aftermath of a bombing raid. Most harrowing is the The Holocaust exhibition, not considered suitable for children under 14.

The narrative collection is brilliantly chosen, containing many personal and everyday objects from the trenches, the concentration camps, the Far East, the Eastern Front, the Atlantic Ocean and all the significant theatres of war. These are combined with memorabilia such as recruiting posters, dramatic contemporary film footage and spoken first-hand accounts from ordinary combatants and survivors.

Conflicts since 1945 are also well handled and the Secret War Exhibition, detailing clandestine operations from World War I to the present day, is fascinating. The top floor features the gallery, Crimes Against Humanity, considered suitable for over 12s.

www.iwm.org.uk

✚ 19G (off map) ✉ Lambeth Road ☎ 020 7416 5000 🕐 Daily 10–6. Closed 24–26 Dec 👤 Free 🍴 Café (£) Ⓜ Lambeth North, Elephant & Castle, Waterloo, Southwark

JEWEL TOWER

This solitary tower is one of the few remaining parts of the old Palace of Westminster (➤ 41). Built in 1366, it was used to house the personal valuables of Edward III and was known as the Royal Wardrobe. Today it makes an excellent introduction to the Houses of Parliament with an exhibition about their history and procedural practices. You can also take a 'tour' of Parliament on a multimedia touch-screen.

www.english-heritage.org.uk

🕇 12D ✉ Old Palace Yard, Abingdon Street ☎ 020 7222 2219 🕐 Apr–Oct daily 10–5; Nov–Mar 10–4 👪 Inexpensive 🍴 Westminster Arms (£), Storey's Gate 🚇 Westminster, St James's Park

LONDON COUNTY HALL AND SEA LIFE LONDON AQUARIUM

In London's former County Hall are several attractions for teenagers looking for a fun day out. The SEA LIFE London Aquarium is the capital's major aquarium and has 14 themed zones, ending with the Shark Walk Finale, where you can walk across a glass floor looking down at the denizens of the deep. Namco Station has 150 interactive video games, 12 lanes of Techno Bowling and bumper cars; The Movieum goes behind the scenes in the film industry. Unashamedly scary is Fright Club, more educational are the Dalí Universe, an exhibition dedicated to the Spanish Surrealist painter.

www.londoncountyhall.com; **www.**sealife.co.uk/london

🕇 16G ✉ County Hall, Westminster Bridge Road ☎ 0871 663 1678 🕐 Aquarium: Mon–Fri 10–5, Sat, Sun 10–6 (last admission one hour before closing); other attractions: check website 👪 Expensive 🍴 Café next door 🚇 Westminster

LONDON DUNGEON

'Abandon hope all who enter here' is the message of the London Dungeon, the world's first and foremost museum of medieval (and other) horrors. It was begun in 1975 by a London housewife whose children were disappointed by the lack of blood and gore on display at the Tower of London. The dark tunnels beneath London Bridge now include many more blood-curdling special effects, with a 'dark ride' (in every sense) and costumed actors to enhance the scream factor. Ghouls and the curious, including most of London's overseas teenagers, make this one of the capital's most visited attractions, but this is definitely not a place for young children or the faint of heart.

www.thedungeons.com

✚ 22H ✉ Tooley Street ☎ 020 7403 7221 (general enquiries)
🕔 Varies year-round between 9:30 and 7. Check by phone. Closed 25
Dec ✋ Very expensive 🍴 Butler's Wharf Chop House (££; ➤ 58)
Ⓛ London Bridge

LONDON EYE

This giant landmark wheel was erected as part of the capital's Millennium celebrations and quickly became one of the hottest attraction tickets in town. Its 32 observation capsules soar majestically 135m (443ft) directly above the Thames, making it the tallest wheel of its kind in the world. A full revolution takes 30 minutes, offering magnificent views right across the heart of central London and far beyond.

A limited number of seats is available to those who show up in person (these are quickly snapped up); the rest are reserved by telephone. The best advice is to reserve well ahead. Boarding takes around 30 minutes.

www.londoneye.com

✚ 16G ✉ Riverside Gardens, next to County Hall ☎ 0870 500 0600
🕐 May, Jun daily 10–9; Jul, Aug 10–9:30; Sep 10–9; Oct–Apr 10–8
🎟 Expensive 🍴 Riverfront cafés 🚇 Waterloo

OXO TOWER

Built in 1930 for the Oxo food product company, this splendid art deco tower has long been a Thames landmark, but had fallen into such disrepair that demolition was likely. Lovingly restored, its huge illuminated red O X O trademark letters make it one of the most striking sights on the London night skyline. The tower houses exhibition spaces, restaurants (open daily), award-winning craft and designer shops and studios. There are panoramic views from the free 8th-floor public viewing gallery.

www.coinstreet.org

✚ 18J ✉ Oxo Tower Wharf, Barge House Street, South Bank ☎ 020 7401 1686 🕐 Viewing gallery 11–10 🎟 Free 🚇 Blackfriars, Waterloo

SHAKESPEARE'S GLOBE

For many, the highlight of a London visit during the summer months is watching a Shakespearean play in the sort of setting that the Bard himself might recognize: a circular theatre, open to the sky, built from oak and roofed with water reed thatch. Sit in the galleries, or, for an authentic, cheaper but more tiring experience, stand in the Yard for £5.

The Globe Exhibition, telling the story behind this remarkable project, features a major exhibition on the world of Shakespeare and includes a theatrical tour (year-round).

www.shakespeares-globe.org

✚ 20J ✉ 21 New Globe Walk, Bankside ☎ 020 7902 1400 🕓 Daily 9–5. Closed 24–25 Dec
🍴 Bar (£), Brasserie (££) 🚇 Mansion House, Southwark, London Bridge ♿ Expensive
❓ Guided tours. Performances May–Oct ☎ 020 7401 9919

SOUTHWARK CATHEDRAL

Often overlooked by visitors, Southwark Cathedral boasts one of the oldest and most interesting church interiors in the capital. Construction began in 1220 and was finished some 200 years later (though most of its exterior features were remodelled much later). The nave retains some original stonework and fascinating 15th-century ornamental carvings – one depicts the devil swallowing Judas Iscariot. There are several grand monuments, the most notable being to the area's most famous parishioner, William Shakespeare, who lived in Southwark from 1599 to 1611. His brother Edmund (died 1607) and other fellow dramatists are buried in the cathedral.

http://cathedral.southwark.anglican.org

✚ 21H ✉ Cathedral Street ☎ 020 7367 6700 ⏰ Daily 8–6 ✋ Tour inexpensive 🍴 Café/restaurant (£) in refectory 🚇 London Bridge

TATE BRITAIN

Opened in 1897 as the National Gallery of British Art, Tate Britain is now one of four Tate galleries. What was originally a collection donated to the nation by sugar magnate Sir Henry Tate has mushroomed into the largest array of British art in the world, from the 16th century to the present day. This grand building is the original home of the collection; the other three galleries are Tate Modern (► 123), Tate Liverpool and Tate St Ives in Cornwall. Since entry is free, you can take your time. Rather than wander aimlessly, it might be worth choosing a favourite historic period or artist. Painters well represented include William Hogarth, Sir Joshua Reynolds, Thomas Gainsborough, William Blake and John Constable; the Clore Gallery features some 300 paintings by J M W Turner. Or look at more recent British stars, such as sculptors Barbara Hepworth and Henry Moore.
www.tate.org.uk/britain

⊞ 11B ⊠ Millbank ☎ 020 7887 8888 ⏰ Daily 10–5:50 (also first Fri in month 6pm–10pm). Closed 24–26 Dec ✋ Free (charge for exhibitions)
🍴 Tate Britain Café (£); Rex Whistler Restaurant (£££) ☎ 020 7887 8825
🚇 Pimlico, Vauxhall ❓ Free guided tours daily. Audio guides (inexpensive). Art Trolley activities for children (aged 5+) Sun 11–5. During gallery opening hours, the Tate Boat runs every 40 min between Tate Britain and Tate Modern

TATE MODERN

No museum has altered British attitudes to art more than Tate Modern, London's first new museum for over a century. When it opened in 2000, some six million visitors explored what had been a disused power station. Instead of tearing it down, architects opened up the vast turbine hall that now houses ever-changing and always controversial exhibits. Now it is the most popular gallery of modern art in the world.

Although the bedrock of the Tate collection is British art, Tate Modern has one of the world's finest collections of international modern and contemporary works since 1900. From the Fauves onwards, the list is dazzling, from Picasso and Matisse to Surrealists such as Dalí, Magritte and Miró. Familiar works by Abstract Expressionists such as Jackson Pollock feature, as well as Pop Art by Lichtenstein and Warhol. Take a break in the top floor café with its views over the St Paul's Cathedral and the Thames.
www.tate.org.uk/modern

✚ 20H ✉ Bankside ☎ 020 7887 8888 🕓 Sun–Thu 10–6, Fri, Sat 10–10 (last admission 45 mins before closing) 🚻 Free 🍴 Tate Modern Café (£), Tate Modern Restaurant (£££) 🚇 Southwark, Mansion House, St Paul's ❓ Daily guided tours (free). Audio guides (inexpensive). Footbridge from St Paul's Cathedral. During gallery opening hours, the Tate Boat runs every 40 min between Tate Modern and Tate Britain

WESTMINSTER ABBEY
Best places to see, pages 54–55.

WESTMINSTER CATHEDRAL
Not to be confused with the more illustrious abbey of the same name, Westminster Cathedral is London's principal Roman Catholic church. Its foundation is relatively modern: it was built between 1896 and 1903. The Byzantine campanile (accessible by elevator) is one of the capital's lesser-known landmarks, towering some 83m (273ft) high and offering great views over central London. The cathedral interior is famous for some of the finest and most varied marble-work in the country, though it has never been completed and much of the huge nave ceiling still shows bare brickwork.

www.westminstercathedral.org.uk

🕂 10C 🖂 Victoria Street ☎ 020 7798 9055 🕔 Mon–Fri 7–7, Sat, Sun 8–7. Tower: Apr–Nov daily 9:30–12:30, 1–5; Dec–Mar Thu–Sun 9–5 ✋ Cathedral free (donations appreciated); tower moderate 🚇 Victoria

HOTELS

London County Hall Travel Inn (£)

The most economical, central base for a family stay in London, right below the London Eye (➤ 118–119), cheek by jowl with SEA LIFE London Aquarium (➤ 116) and the other County Hall attractions. It is just a stroll across the bridge from the Houses of Parliament and Big Ben.

✉ Belvedere Road ☎ 0870 238 3300; www.premierinn.com 🚇 Waterloo, Westminster

Mad Hatter Hotel (££)

Close to Shakespeare's Globe, Tate Modern and the London Eye, this hotel is set in a former 19th-century millinery factory. Modern bedrooms; traditional British dishes in restaurant.

✉ 3–7 Stamford Street ☎ 020 7401 9222; www.fullershotels.com
🚇 Waterloo

RESTAURANTS

Butlers Wharf Chop House (££)

See page 58.

Livebait (£–££)

Lively, informal seafood restaurant where the décor is simple and the standard of cooking and service is high.

✉ 43 The Cut ☎ 020 7928 7211 🕐 Mon–Sat 12–11, Sun 12:30–9
🚇 Waterloo, Southwark

Oxo Tower Brasserie (££–£££)

Not to be confused with the Oxo Tower Restaurant, the bright brasserie also has wonderful views over London. There are plenty of outdoor tables and an interesting European menu, more wide-ranging than the word 'brasserie' implies. The bar is good for pre-dinner drinks, cocktails or lighter snacks. Live jazz is a regular feature.

✉ Oxo Tower Wharf, Barge House Street ☎ 020 7803 3888 🕐 Daily lunch, dinner 🚇 Southwark, Waterloo

SHOPPING

Bermondsey (New Caledonian) Market

London's prime market for serious antiques collectors and the trade, who snap up most of the bargains very early. There are also some good antiques shops that stay open all week.

✉ Bermondsey Square ☎ http://bermondseysquare.co.uk/antiques.html
🕐 Fri 4am–1pm (starts closing at noon) 🚇 London Bridge

ENTERTAINMENT

THEATRE, MUSIC AND DANCE

St John's

This deconsecrated baroque church makes a superb setting for concerts, mostly of chamber music. The lunchtime concerts every other Thursday are excellent value.

✉ Smith Square ☎ 020 7222 1061; www.sjss.org.uk 🚇 Westminster

Southbank Centre

The Royal Festival Hall, the Hayward Gallery and the Queen Elizabeth Hall, with its Purcell Room are all parts of the Southbank Centre, an arts complex dating from the 1950s. The venues of the Southbank Centre host arts for all: classical and world music, rock and pop, jazz and dance, comedy and poetry, and, in the Hayward Gallery, the changing exhibitions of the visual arts.

✉ Southbank Centre, Belvedere Road ☎ 0871 663 2501; box office: 0871 663 2500; www.southbankcentre.co.uk 🕐 Hayward Gallery: Sat–Thu 10–6, Fri 10–10; other venues: check website 🚇 Waterloo, Embankment

(Royal) National Theatre

The 'National' is much admired for the outstanding quality of the serious work it produces in its three theatres: the Olivier, the Lyttleton or the Cottesloe. All have productions in repertory and you can also take backstage tours.

✉ South Bank ☎ Box office: 020 7452 3000; information and backstage tours: 020 7452 3400; www.nationaltheatre.org.uk 🚇 Embankment, Waterloo, Covent Garden ❓ A few discounted tickets for 'sell-out' productions are on sale on the day of performance from 9:30am onwards. Get there early as they sell out quickly

Knightsbridge, Kensington and Chelsea

Once remote from the City of London, these premier residential districts and former villages were favoured for their healthy air well away from the pollution of early London.

Today they retain their exclusivity with their grand Georgian houses and leafy squares that have attracted the wealthy and have become home to several embassies and consulates. Kensington gained its fashionable reputation in the late 17th century when the Royal Family moved to Kensington Palace. Popular with sightseers and shoppers is South Kensington, where there are museums containing some of the best collections of arts and crafts, science and natural history in the world. Next is Knightsbridge, an even more exclusive address, whose affluent residents use the world-famous Harrods department store as their local shop. Most visitors are happy just to gaze at the richness and variety of the stock, the lavish interiors and tempting food halls. To the south is the more bohemian Chelsea. Still a classy and incredibly expensive area in which to live, it is still synonymous with 'London's Swinging 60s' and popular for shopping in the lively King's Road.

APSLEY HOUSE

Apsley House, also known as the Wellington Museum, was the London home of Arthur Wellesley, first Duke of Wellington, from 1829 until his death in 1852. Wellington was the greatest soldier of his day, achieving major military successes in India, Spain and Portugal before crowning his career with the defeat of Napoleon at Waterloo in 1815.

The museum is divided into two parts. Collections of plates and china, magnificent table centrepieces, swords, medals and so on relate to the Duke's adventures, and there is also an outstanding picture collection with 200 works by Spanish and Italian old masters. But, the most memorable piece is a heroic nude statue of Napoleon by Canova (commissioned by the Little Emperor himself) in which he is depicted as a god.

www.english-heritage.org.uk

➕ 8E ✉ 149 Piccadilly, Hyde Park Corner ☎ 020 7499 5676 🕔 Apr–Oct
Wed–Sun 11–5 (last admission 4:30);
Nov–Mar 11–4. Closed 24–26 Dec, 1 Jan
✋ Moderate 🍴 Pizza on the Park (£), 11–13
Knightsbridge, 020 7235 7825 🚇 Hyde Park
Corner

CHELSEA

One of London's most fashionable suburbs in every sense, Chelsea was synonymous with both London's 'Swinging 60s' and the late 1970s punk rock movement. The latter began at SEX, still a fashion boutique at 430

King's Road. Today it is more classy though still lively and is best explored on foot (▶ 130–131).

➕ 4A

HARRODS

Harrods is much more than just a shop: it is an internationally famous institution and even the most reluctant shopper should venture into its cathedral-like portals. The store began trading here in 1849 as a small, family-run grocery shop and by 1911 the present magnificent building was complete. Occupying over 1.8ha (4.5 acres), it is Britain's biggest department store. Among the highlights are the stylish Food Halls. The Meat Hall is gloriously decorated with 1902 tiles, while the fresh-fish display is an extravaganza of the bounty of the sea.

www.harrods.com

➕ 6D ✉ 87–135 Brompton Road ☎ 020 7730 1234 🕐 Mon–Sat 10–8, Sun 11:30–6 🍴 Variety in store (£–£££) Ⓜ Knightsbridge ❓ No one admitted wearing scruffy clothes, tank tops (men), short shorts or cycling shorts. Backpacks to be left in lockers. Charge for toilets

a walk around Chelsea

Start from Sloane Square underground station.

Walk straight ahead to King's Road. Turn left through an arch to Duke of York Square.

This former army barracks now houses shops, cafés and the Saatchi Gallery(➤ 135).

*Pass the gallery; turn left into Cheltenham Terrace, then right into St Leonard's Terrace. Turn left into Durham Place. At the end is the 300-year-old **Royal Hospital**.*

In this retirement home for 'Chelsea pensioners', ex-soldiers wear traditional scarlet uniforms.

Cross Royal Hospital Road to visit the grounds, or turn right for the National Army Museum (➤ 134). Continue on Royal Hospital Road; turn left into Tite Street.

Former residents include Oscar Wilde (No 34), and painter John Singer Sargent (No 31).

Turn right onto Dilke Street.

At the end is a must for garden lovers. The 17th-century Chelsea Physic Garden helped to train apprentice apothecaries to recognize medicinal plants.

Turn left into Swan Walk. At the end, across the river, is the Peace Pagoda, a gift from Japan. Turn right on Chelsea Embankment; continue to Cheyne Walk, sheltered by gardens from the traffic.

Plaques mark the homes of novelist George Elliot (No 4), painter Dante Gabriel Rossetti and poet Algernon Swinburne (both No 16).

Continue past Albert Bridge to Chelsea Old Church, with its fine tombs.

The statue outside is of the Sir Thomas More, who lived here (1520–1535).

Turn immediately right into Old Church Street, past The Pig's Ear pub and rejoin King's Road. Turn right and return to Sloane Square past tempting boutiques.

Distance 5–6km (3–3.75 miles)
Time 2–6 hours depending on visits
Start/end point 🚇 Sloane Square ✚ 7C
Lunch Pig's Ear (£–££) ✉ 35 Old Church Street
☎ 020 7352 2908

Royal Hospital, Chelsea ☎ 020 7881 5200
🕐 Daily 10–12, 2–4. Closed Sun Oct–Mar 🎟 Free

Chelsea Physic Garden ☎ 020 7352 5646 🕐 Apr–Oct Wed 12–5,
Sun 2–6 🍴 Café (£) 🎟 Moderate

HYDE PARK

The largest and most famous of central London's open spaces, Hyde Park covers 142ha (350 acres) and was once the royal hunting ground of Henry VIII and Elizabeth I.

At its northeast corner, at the very end of Oxford Street, is Marble Arch; it was originally erected in front of Buckingham Palace but was moved as a result of palace redevelopment. Nearby is Speakers' Corner, London's most famous 'soapbox' where anyone may air their views (within reason).

Flowing through the park is the Serpentine lake, created in 1730, and just west of here is the **Serpentine Gallery**, featuring revolving exhibitions of contemporary art. Across the road is the sculptural Princess Diana Memorial Fountain, which was opened in 2004 by the Queen.

www.royalparks.gov.uk

➕ 5F ☎ 020 7298 2100 (Park Office) 🕐 Daily 5am–midnight ✋ Free
🚇 Marble Arch, Knightsbridge, Hyde Park Corner

Serpentine Gallery

☎ 020 7402 6075; www.serpentinegallery.org 🕐 Daily 10–6 during exhibitions ✋ Free 🚇 Lancaster Gate, South Kensington

KENSINGTON PALACE AND GARDENS

William III was the first monarch to set up home in Kensington Palace, in 1689, and it was here in 1819 that the future Queen Victoria was born. Royal patronage continues with several members of the present royal family having palace apartments. In September 1997 it was a focus of the country's grief as the last home of the late Princess Diana, when thousands of floral tributes were piled up in front of the palace gates. There is no memorial within the palace to Diana but a memorial playground is close by in Kensington Gardens (► 68).

The fabric of the present palace, which actually resembles a country house in both style and size, dates largely from the early 18th century. One highlight is the display of Princess Diana's gowns, including the dark blue silk velvet worn when she danced with John Travolta at the White House in 1985. Another is the bedroom where 18-year-old Princess Victoria woke up in 1837 to learn that her uncle had died and that she was now Queen Victoria. Surrounding the palace are fine sunken gardens and an orangery, now a restaurant.

Outside the palace gates is Kensington Gardens, which runs east into Hyde Park. This pretty lawned expanse boasts two famous statues. To the east is Peter Pan, and to the southeast,

near the Royal Albert Hall, is the amazingly intricate 53m-high (174ft) Albert Memorial, which is dedicated to Prince Albert, Queen Victoria's consort.

www.hrp.org.uk

🔲 3F 🖂 Kensington Gardens ☎ 0844 482 7777 🕓 Daily Mar–Oct 10–6 (last admission 5); Nov–Feb 10–5 (last admission 4). Closed 24–26 Dec 🔱 Expensive 🍴 The Orangery (£–££) 🔵 High Street Kensington, Queensway 🔢 Audio guide included in ticket price

LEIGHTON HOUSE

The distinguished Victorian artist Frederic Lord Leighton (1830–96) created this beautiful romantic house between 1864 and 1866 and lived here until his death in 1896. The centrepiece is the Arab Hall, a glorious mini-Alhambra featuring a dome from Damascus, window screens from Cairo and Leighton's rare collection of 15th- and 16th-century Islamic tiles from Cairo, Damascus and Rhodes. The other rooms are much more restrained but contain some fine works by Lord Leighton and his famous Pre-Raphaelite associates.

www.rbkc.gov.uk

🕂 1D (off map) ✉ 12 Holland Park Road ☎ 020 7602 3316 🕓 Wed–Mon 11–5:30. Closed 25–26 Dec, 1 Jan ✋ Moderate 🍴 Several on High Street Kensington (£–££) 🚇 High Street Kensington

NATIONAL ARMY MUSEUM

The first professional British Army was formed in 1485 and this museum, refurbished and upgraded, covers its history in the five centuries to date. Audiovisual presentations, dioramas and lifelike soldier mannequins bring to life the lot of the ordinary soldier in a manner that concentrates more on the daily hardships than on the glory of war.

Start in the basement with the Making of Britain, which moves from Agincourt to the American War of Independence. As well as admiring the fine display of swords you can try on a civil war helmet and feel the weight of a cannon shot. The Road to Waterloo follows the story of the soldiers in Wellington's army and includes a huge, scale model of the battlefield (at the critical moment of 7.15pm on 18 June, 1815) and the skeleton of Napoleon's beloved war horse, Marengo. Displays on the two World Wars and the modern British Army (1965 to date) bring the story up to date.

www.national-army-museum.ac.uk

🚇 6A ✉ Royal Hospital Road, Chelsea ☎ 020 7730 0717; 020 7881 2455 (info line) 🕐 Daily 10–5:30. Closed 24–26 Dec, 1 Jan, Good Fri, May Day ✋ Free 🍴 Café (£) Ⓢ Sloane Square ❓ Self-guiding tours available

NATURAL HISTORY MUSEUM
Best places to see, pages 44–45.

SAATCHI GALLERY
Glass and steel has transformed this 200-year-old former military building into arguably the most exciting cutting-edge art gallery in Britain. Expect to see works by avant-garde international artists or young artists that have yet to make an impact.

www.saatchi-gallery.co.uk

🚇 6B ✉ Duke of York's HQ, King's Road ☎ 020 7823 2363 🕐 Daily 10–6 ✋ Free 🍴 Mess café (£) Ⓢ Sloane Square

SCIENCE MUSEUM
Best places to see, ➤ 48–49.

V&A
Best places to see, ➤ 52–53.

HOTELS

Avonmore Hotel (£)

A privately owned, AA award-winning B&B offers single, double and triple rooms and a friendly atmosphere.

✉ 66 Avonmore Road, Kensington ☎ 020 7603 3121; www.avonmorehotel.co.uk 🚇 West Kensington

base2stay (£)

Small but practical rooms, plain decoration, mini-kitchens: this is affordable accommodation par excellence. Walking distance to Tube station, shops, pubs and cafés.

✉ 25 Courtfield Gardens ☎ 020 7244 2255; www.base2stay.com 🚇 Earl's Court

Beaufort (££)

The small Beaufort hotel, in a quiet tree-lined square near Harrods, is comfortably furnished with lots of individual extras.

✉ 33 Beaufort Gardens ☎ 020 3355 9452; www.thebeaufort.co.uk 🚇 Knightsbridge

Byron (££)

A charming terraced house, thoughtfully restored. Bedrooms are comfortable and tastefully furnished.

✉ 36–38 Queensborough Terrace ☎ 020 7243 0987; www.thebyronhotel.co.uk 🚇 Queensway

Delmere (£)

Smart, friendly staff, well-equipped rooms and a jazz-themed bar are the main attractions of this boutique hotel near Hyde Park.

✉ 130 Sussex Gardens ☎ 020 7706 3344; www.delmerehotels.com 🚇 Paddington

easyHotel (£)

Part of a chain started by Stelios and using the easyJet formula, this hotel promises cheerful, simple accommodation. The earlier you book, the cheaper it is. Close to the Natural History Museum as well as Kensington and Knightsbridge galleries and shops.

✉ 14 Lexham Gardens ☎ 020 7216 1717; www.easyhotel.com ⓔ Earl's Court, Gloucester Road

London Vicarage Hotel (£)

This Victorian townhouse is an affordable, family-run B&B set on a quiet square. Handy for Kensington High Street. Free WiFi, but no elevators.

✉ 10 Vicarage Gate ☎ 020 7229 4030; www.londonvicaragehotel.com ⓔ High Street Kensington, Notting Hill Gate

Mitre House Hotel (£)

This is a long-established hotel with comfortable, well-furnished rooms that offer good facilities. Close to Hyde Park.

✉ 178–186 Sussex Gardens ☎ 020 7723 8040; www.mitrehousehotel.com ⓔ Lancaster Gate

Morgan House Hotel (£)

In a Georgian townhouse, this personally-run B&B has budget-friendly prices for a mix of rooms both with and without private bathrooms. Handy for major sightseeing attractions.

✉ 120 Ebury Street ☎ 020 7730 2384; www.morganhouse.co.uk ⓔ Victoria

RESTAURANTS

Al Bustan (££)

The name means garden in Arabic and greenery abounds in this classy, formal Lebanese restaurant. The food is authentic and very tasty.

✉ 68 Old Brompton Road ☎ 020 7584 5805 🕐 Daily 12–10:30 ⓔ South Kensington

Amaya (££)

Not the cheapest Indian restaurant in London, but the setting is chic and modern, the dishes are authentic and the ingredients luxurious: lobster, leg of lamb, duck, venison, oysters. Much is prepared on a charcoal grill, griddle or in the tandoor clay oven.

✉ Halkin Arcade, 15 Motcomb Street ☎ 020 7823 1166 🕐 Daily lunch, dinner ⓔ Knightsbridge

Bluebird (£–£££)

This King's Road 'Gastrodome' comprises an alfresco café, a lively flower market and an excellent food shop, while the floor above is home to the Bluebird restaurant, which serves an eclectic range of Modern European cuisine and great cocktails.

✉ 350 King's Road, Chelsea ☎ 020 7559 1000 🕒 Daily breakfast, lunch, dinner 🚇 Sloane Square then 🚌 19, 22

The Orangery (£–££)

Serving late breakfasts, elegant lunches and traditional English afternoon teas, the 18th-century Orangery restaurant is a stylish oasis in Kensington Palace. Admission to the palace is not required to eat here.

✉ Kensington Palace ☎ 020 3166 6115 🕒 Daily Mar–Oct 10–6, Nov–Feb 10–5 🚇 High Street Kensington, Notting Hill Gate

Pig's Ear (£–££)

Just off Chelsea's King's Road, this gastropub combines groovy cocktails with Modern European classics such as confit pork belly, braised lamb shank, chocolate bread and butter pudding. Good cheeseboard.

✉ 5 Old Church Street ☎ 020 7352 2908 🕒 Mon–Sat noon–11pm, Sun noon–10:30 🚇 Sloane Square

Poissonerie de l'Avenue (££)

Long-established fish specialist with a menu that seems unchanged for decades: oysters and escargots, coquilles Saint-Jacques, lobster Thermidor, Sole Véronique.

✉ 82 Sloane Avenue ☎ 020 7589 2457 🕒 Daily lunch, dinner 🚇 South Kensington, Sloane Square

Racine (££)

It doesn't get more Gallic in London than this popular Knightsbridge brasserie just opposite the South Kensington museums. Expect hearty bourgeois fare with big flavours.

✉ 239 Brompton Road ☎ 020 7584 4477 🕒 Daily lunch, dinner 🚇 South Kensington

Wódka (£–££)

Polish food with a modern twist served with some style as it has been for 20 years. Well-priced lunch menus, three small tables outdoors in summer.

✉ 12 St Alban's Grove ☎ 020 7937 6513 🕓 Lunch Tue–Fri; dinner daily; Sun brunch 🚇 High Street Kensington

SHOPPING

ANTIQUES

Alfies Antique Market

Some 80 dealers under one roof offer everything from clothes and posters to 20th-century collectables. There is a fun rooftop café.

✉ 13–25 Church Street ☎ 020 7723 6066 🚇 Edgware Road

Chelsea Antiques Market

Claimed to be the oldest antiques market in Britain. The dealers here cover most interests and at prices that are relatively good value compared to the King's Road.

✉ 245a–253 King's Road ☎ 020 7352 5689 🚇 Sloane Square

Portobello Road Market

This market is fun most days, but it is crammed on Saturdays when 1,000 registered antiques dealers set up their stalls at dawn.

✉ Portobello Road and environs 🕓 General market: Mon–Wed, Fri, Sat 8–6:30, Thu 8–1. Antiques: Sat 5:30am–6pm 🚇 Notting Hill Gate

DEPARTMENT STORES

Harrods

London's ultimate shopping experience (➤ 129).

✉ 87–135 Brompton Road, Knightsbridge ☎ 020 7730 1234
🚇 Knightsbridge ❓ Dress code: no scruffy attire, very short or cycling shorts

Harvey Nichols

Worth looking at for its renowned window displays this is the favourite shop of London's rich young things but also has a good menswear department and a mouth-watering food hall.

✉ 109–125 Knightsbridge ☎ 020 7235 5000 🚇 Knightsbridge

Peter Jones

One of London's most elegant stores, this is one of the John Lewis chain of department stores. It is known for its helpful staff as well as a wide range on seven light, airy floors: clothes, beauty products, china and glass, jewellery, toys and more.

✉ Sloane Square ☎ 020 7730 3434; www.peterjones.co.uk
Ⓤ Sloane Square

The Shop at Bluebird

This huge space displays edgy fashion and accessories, handbags and shoes, furniture and stuffed animals. Expect the unexpected.

✉ 350 King's Road ☎ 020 7351 3873 Ⓤ Sloane Square

DESIGN AND FURNISHINGS
Conran Shop

Let style guru Sir Terence Conran counsel you on household accessories, furniture and food. The shop is worth a visit for the splendid art deco building which also houses Bibendum, an expensive restaurant.

✉ Michelin House, 81 Fulham Road ☎ 020 7589 7401 Ⓒ Daily (Sun 12–6)
Ⓤ South Kensington

General Trading Company

This company has been going since 1920, and is credited with the concept of the 'wedding list'. The whole place is laid out like a stylish home stocking furniture, tableware and gifts.

✉ 2 Symons Street ☎ 020 7730 0411 Ⓒ Mon–Sat 10–7, Sun 11–5:30
Ⓤ Sloane Square

ENTERTAINMENT

The Royal Albert Hall

Since 1871, this grand Victorian 5,500-seat hall has hosted everything from classical concerts to boxing championships, from rock 'n' roll to tennis. The annual highlight is the BBC Promenade season, with 75 concerts (mid-July to mid-September).

✉ Kensington Gore ☎ 0845 401 5045; www.royalalberthall.com
Ⓤ High Street Kensington

Covent Garden, Bloomsbury and Soho

This is an area of contrasts with some of London's most visited sights within its boundaries. Its character dramatically changes within the space of a few streets, from bookshops to street markets, from residential to retail and from busy and vibrant to genteel and peaceful.

Covent Garden is the site of London's former wholesale fruit and vegetable market, now located south of the Thames. After its

move the whole area took on a new character and visitors flock to its shops, market stalls, bars, cafés and restaurants. It is a top spot for free street entertainment – on any one day you might hear a talented violinist, watch a clown, see magic tricks or stop to gaze at one of the 'living' statues.

West of Covent Garden are Chinatown and Soho, a hive of activity, full of restaurants, bars and clubs. Just a few minutes' travel to the north and you are in the sedate and genteel Bloomsbury. The houses are elegant, the atmosphere literate. Here the finest of collections is housed at the British Museum. To the west are more fine buildings and attractions including Madame Tussauds waxworks and famous paintings in the Wallace Collection.

BRITISH MUSEUM
Best places to see, ➤ 36–37.

CARTOON MUSEUM
Spend a chuckle-inducing hour at this collection of original cartoons and caricatures, cartoon strips and comics. On display are over 250 original cartoons, caricatures and comics by top cartoonists and leading artists from the past. There is a reference library open by appointment with some 4,000 books on cartoons, as well as a collection of 2,500 comics, and the museum hosts regular cartoon-related events. A room on the top floor provides youngsters with paper, crayons and tips on cartooning.
www.cartoonmuseum.org

🔒 15L 📧 35 Little Russell Street ☎ 020 7580 8155
🕐 Tue–Sat 10:30–5:30, Sun 12–5:30 💷 Moderate
🚇 Holborn, Tottenham Court Road

COVENT GARDEN
Best places to see, ➤ 38–39.

LONDON TRANSPORT MUSEUM
From the sedan chairs of 1800 to the World Cities Gallery, showing how urban populations commute in the 21st century, the story here is about social history, technology and transport. See how the world's first underground railway was built in London, watch film footage of women, who kept the buses and tube running during World War II, and peer at the original design for the tube map, drawn by Harry Beck in 1933. The stars of the museum are the historic vehicles, from a horse-drawn bus to a steam-driven train that ran underground, and from a 1904 taxi to a number 11 red double-

decker bus. Children will love to climb aboard a trolley or a tram, and to 'drive' a Jubilee Line Tube train on the simulator.

www.ltmcollection.org

🚲 16J 🖂 Covent Garden ☎ 020 7379 6344 🕐 Sat–Thu 10–6 (last admission 5:15), Fri 11–6 🖐 Moderate 🚇 Covent Garden, Charing Cross

a walk around Covent Garden

This walk can take a full day, thanks to the irresistible shops and attractions along the way.

Leave Leicester Square underground station via Charing Cross Road exit; walk south towards Trafalgar Square; turn left into pedestrianized Cecil Court. At the end of Cecil Court, cross St Martin's Lane and enter the tiny alley to the left of the Green Man & French Horn pub.

In the oldest residential part of Covent Garden, this dark alleyway is flanked with 18th-century bow-windowed houses.

At the end, turn left into Bedfordbury, then immediately right into New Row, another pedestrianized street with small shops and restaurants. Go straight ahead, crossing Garrick Street; continue on King Street.

As you enter Covent Garden's west piazza, the portico of St Paul's Church (▶ 39) is on your right. This is where Eliza Doolittle sold violets in the musical *My Fair Lady*.

Keep to the left of the piazza; turn left onto busy James Street, with its cheerful shops and crowds watching the 'human statues'. At Covent Garden underground station, cross Long Acre into Neal Street, another lively pedestrianized street, with shops selling trendy clothes and music. Cross Shelton Street, then turn left into Short's Gardens.

Look up. High on your right, above the Holland & Barrett health-food shop, is an unusual clock, where the hands and bells are powered by water.

Turn right into brightly painted, flowery Neal's Yard.

This oasis retains the 1970s hippy feeling of an urban village with its whole food cafés and alternative therapy shops. Relax over a coffee or herbal tea.

Retrace your steps to Covent Garden underground station on the Piccadilly Line.

Distance 3–4km (2–2.5 miles)
Time 1 hour without stops
Start point 🚇 Leicester Square ➕ 15J
End point 🚇 Covent Garden ➕ 16K
Lunch World Food Café ✉ 14 Neal's Yard (£) ☎ 020 7379 0298

MADAME TUSSAUD'S

The grand old dame of London tourism, Madame T's is infamous for its queues (avoid by booking in advance), as for the excellence of its lifelike figures. Madame Tussaud began her career making death masks of guillotine victims, moved to England in 1802 and set up in London in 1835. You can still see objects of the French Revolution, including the waxworks' oldest figure – Madame Dubarry (Louis XV's mistress), made in 1763. She is cast as The Sleeping Beauty, with an ingenious breathing mechanism to keep her slumbering eternally. You can't touch her, but you can give Brad Pitt a squeeze or make J-Lo blush and the interactive theme continues, allowing you to become a star on Big Brother. There's a special Spiderman feature too, and a Pirates of the Caribbean set with figures of Johnny Depp, Orlando Bloom and Keira Knightley.

The World Stage brings together politicians and royalty, while The Chamber Live is more horrible than ever with live actors to incite even more shock factor (unsuitable for under 12s). Far better to whisk younger children off on the enjoyable Disney-like Spirit of London ride, replete with animatronic figures and special effects.
www.madametussauds.com/london

🔢 26R ✉ Marylebone Road ☎ 0870 999 0046 🕐 Daily 9:30–5:30; longer at peak times. Closed 25 Dec 💷 Very expensive 🍴 Café (£) 🚇 Baker Street
❓ To avoid waiting in line book in advance online

REGENT'S PARK

Like many of London's parks, this land was appropriated by Henry VIII as a royal hunting ground and was not known as Regent's Park until 1820, when the Prince Regent (the future George IV) decided to develop it as a grand new garden city. His architect, John Nash, was also responsible for much of the magnificent building of Bath

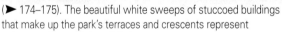

(► 174–175). The beautiful white sweeps of stuccoed buildings that make up the park's terraces and crescents represent only a small part of the original plans, but they remain the most elegant example of town planning in the capital.

The delightful gardens are famous for the Zoo, Queen Mary's Rose Garden and the Regent's Park Open Air Theatre (► 156). You can also go boating on the lake.

www.royalparks.org.uk

✚ 26T 🚾 Free 🚇 South: Regent's Park, Baker Street. North: Camden Town

SHERLOCK HOLMES MUSEUM

This museum is dedicated to the life and times of the fictional detective. Great lengths have been taken to furnish the house exactly as described in Conan Doyle's novels. It is visited by aficionados from around the world, all wanting to see 221b Baker Street, one of the world's most famous literary addresses. A shop sells Holmes memorabilia.

www.sherlock-holmes.co.uk

🞤 26R ✉ 221b Baker Street ☎ 020 7935 8866 ⏱ Daily 9:30–6
✋ Moderate 🚇 Baker Street

SOHO

Soho, bounded roughly by Oxford Street, Regent Street, Coventry Street/Leicester Square and Charing Cross Road, is central London's most cosmopolitan area. Over the centuries it has accommodated waves of French Huguenot, Italian, Greek and Chinese immigrants, and artists too have long been drawn here, giving Soho its Bohemian reputation. By day, many international film and video companies, as well as advertising agencies have their headquarters here, as well as one-of-a-kind quirky shops. By night the area is known for its many reasonably priced restaurants, its buzzing nightlife, and nearby theatres.

🞤 14K 🚇 Piccadilly Circus, Tottenham Court Road, Oxford Circus

WALLACE COLLECTION

Thanks to the addition of a glass roof over the old courtyard, visitor numbers have tripled at this hidden gem of a museum, just a few steps from Oxford Street. As well as enhancing the splendid collection, this light, airy atrium also boasts a stylish French brasserie in the luxuriant greenery. The building itself is like a small stately home.

The main theme of the collection, the legacy of the inveterate 19th-century collector, Sir Richard Wallace, is French 18th-century art. Downstairs, the André Boulle furniture (including pieces made for the Palace of Versailles), is truly staggering, both in opulence and sheer bulk. Alongside is the best museum collection of Sèvres porcelain in the world. Less well known is the Wallace's magnificent collection of arms and armour – arguably the equal of that in the Tower of London. Upstairs in the picture galleries the Gallic theme continues. The most notable exception is the famous Great Gallery, where, among works by Rubens, Rembrandt, Claude and Velázquez, the star exhibits are the *Laughing Cavalier* by Frans Hals and *Perseus and Andromeda* by Titian.

www.wallacecollection.org

🔲 27Q 📧 Hertford House, Manchester Square ☎ 020 7563 9500 🕐 Daily 10–5 ✋ Free 🍴 Wallace Restaurant (££) 🚇 Bond Street, Baker Street
❓ Free guided tours for groups only

ZSL LONDON ZOO

London Zoo is one of the city's most popular attractions, especially for families. Back in 1828, the Zoological Society of London set this up as the world's first scientific zoo, where animals were studied, rather than kept for the amusement of the public. Now the zoo is known internationally for its work for animal conservation and preservation, with breeding programmes for more than 125 species. Cages are giving way to enclosures with more natural environments. What was the Children's Zoo has been closed, and has been replaced by the more educational and active Animal Adventure, with sights, sounds and even smells to stimulate a greater love of nature.

The zoo is not overly large but it's best to plan your day around the timetable of activities, such as feeding times, talks, shows and the entertaining Animals in Action presentations. Other highlights include the gorillas, the Penguin Pool and the Snowdon Aviary. Note that some of the larger animals, including the elephants and rhinos, have been moved to ZSL Whipsnade Zoo to allow them more space.

www.zsl.org

🚇 25T (off map) ✉ Regent's Park ☎ 020 7722 3333 🕐 Mar–Jun, Sep–Oct daily 10–5:30; Jul–Aug 10–6, Nov–Feb 10–4. Closed 25 Dec 💰 Very expensive 🍴 Four cafés (£) 🚇 Camden Town

HOTELS

Covent Garden Hotel (££)

Hip and stylish, right in the heart of London's West End, this is close to theatres, Soho and some of London's best restaurants, bars and night clubs.

✉ 10 Monmouth Street ☎ 020 7806 1000; www.firmdale.com 🚇 Covent Garden, Leicester Square

myhotel Bloomsbury (£)

Affordable boutique hotel, close to all the West End's major attractions. Expect designer rooms, art and atmosphere, based on the principles of feng shui.

✉ 11–13 Bayley Street, Bedford Square ☎ 020 3004 6000; www.myhotels.com 🚇 Tottenham Court Road, Goodge Street

Radisson Edwardian Mountbatten Hotel (££–£££)

Luxury hotel close to Covent Garden, Soho, Trafalgar Square and Oxford Street, with all their shops, theatres, art galleries and museums within walking distance.

✉ Seven Dials, Covent Garden ☎ 020 7836 4300; www.radissonedwardian.com 🚇 Covent Garden, Tottenham Court Road

RESTAURANTS AND PUBS

Café des Amis (£–££)

Authentic French restaurant upstairs, serving French onion soup, *terrine de campagne, moules marinières,* big salads and omelettes. Wine bar downstairs, with well-priced wines by the glass or bottle.

✉ 11–14 Hanover Place, off Long Acre ☎ 020 7379 3444 🕐 Mon–Sat 12–11:30 🚇 Covent Garden

Cafe España (£)

Expect budget prices and big portions in this popular Spanish eatery, where all the favourites are on the menu: paella, chorizo, tortilla, tapas and affordable Spanish wines.

✉ 63 Old Compton Street ☎ 020 7494 1271 🚇 Piccadilly Circus, Leicester Square, Tottenham Court Road

Cigala (£–££)

In a cool, chic setting, order modern versions of Spanish classics: *albondigas* (meat balls), *bacalao* (salt cod), grilled seafood, stuffed peppers. Excellent tapas, outstanding Spanish wine list.

✉ 54 Lamb's Conduit Street ☎ 020 7405 1717 🕐 Mon–Sat 12–10:45, Sun 12–9:30 🚇 Russell Square, Holborn

Food for Thought (£)

Imaginative dishes at this busy, crowded and long-established vegetarian favourite in Covent Garden range from a gingery Vietnamese vegetable stew and butterbean, leek and mushroom pie to above-average desserts.

✉ 31 Neal Street, Covent Garden ☎ 020 7836 9072 🕐 Mon–Sat 12–8:30, Sun 12–5 🚇 Covent Garden

French House

This pub has been a Soho institution for over 80 years. This is no place for beer drinkers but there is an excellent restaurant upstairs.

✉ 49 Dean Street ☎ 020 7437 2799 🕐 Daily 12–11 (Sun 10:30) 🚇 Leicester Square

Joe Allen (££)

The classic mainstream American food (French toast, burgers, rubs) is served, but it's the celebrities and atmosphere that draw the crowds to this Covent Garden basement.

✉ 13 Exeter Street, Covent Garden ☎ 020 7836 0651 🕐 Daily breakfast, lunch, dinner 🚇 Covent Garden

Lamb and Flag

See page 66.

Loch Fyne (£–££)

One of a successful chain of seafood restaurants, this branch has a well-priced set menu for theatregoers or shoppers. Try the smoked fish pie or the Thai-style squid salad.

✉ 2–4 Catherine Street ☎ 020 7240 4999 🕐 Mon–Sat 12–11, Sun 12–10 🚇 Covent Garden

Masala Zone (£–££)

Dining-hall-style eatery with an easy to negotiate menu providing a top value taste of pan-Indian cooking. There are five other branches in London, including one in Covent Garden.

✉ 9 Marshall Street ☎ 020 7287 9966 🕐 Daily lunch, dinner Ⓤ Oxford Circus

Navarro's (£)

Some of London's best tapas as well as a short menu of full traditional Spanish meals, served in an attractive tiled dining room.

✉ 67 Charlotte Street ☎ 020 7637 7713 🕐 Mon–Fri lunch, Mon–Sat dinner Ⓤ Goodge Street

Providores (££–£££)

Fusion cooking at its best: New Zealand mixed with Asian and Middle Eastern spicing. From roast duck with massaman curry lentils to roast cod on ginger and *wasabi tobikko arancini*.

✉ 109 Marylebone High Street ☎ 020 7935 6175 🕐 Daily 12–2:45, 6–10:30 Ⓤ Baker Street, Bond Street, Regents Park

Rules (£££)

London's oldest restaurant celebrated 200 years in 1998 and still draws plaudits for its top-quality British food.

✉ 35 Maiden Lane, Covent Garden ☎ 020 7836 5314 🕐 Daily lunch, dinner Ⓤ Covent Garden, Charing Cross

Wagamama (£)

This is the original Wagamama noodle bar that now has branches in Covent Garden and worldwide. Food is eaten dining-hall style.

✉ 4 Streatham Street ☎ 020 7323 9223 🕐 Daily lunch, dinner Ⓤ Tottenham Court Road

SHOPPING

BABY ACCESSORIES

Mothercare

This 50-year-old British institution is the market leader, with three floors of everything from babywear and toys to pushchairs.

✉ 526–528 Oxford Street ☎ 020 7629 6621 Ⓤ Marble Arch

BEAUTY AND COSMETICS

Neal's Yard Remedies

The original store in Covent Garden selling essential oils and homeopathic remedies of all kinds.

✉ 15 Neal's Yard ☎ 020 7379 7222 🚇 Covent Garden

Penhaligon's

Beautiful Victorian shopfront and fittings with colognes and powders, perfumes and accessories. Several branches.

✉ 41 Wellington Street ☎ 020 7836 2150 🚇 Covent Garden

BOOKS

Blackwell

Expert staff know every inch of the in-depth sections on history, philosophy, finance, fiction, medical and computing.

✉ 100 Charing Cross Road ☎ 020 7292 5100 🚇 Covent Garden, Tottenham Court Road

Foyles

Despite its apparent disorder, this is the biggest book shop in Britain so you're sure to find what you want here – eventually.

✉ 113–119 Charing Cross Road ☎ 020 7437 5660 🚇 Tottenham Court Road, Covent Garden

Stanford's

The world's largest travel book shop with a vast selection of guides, travelogues and maps to everywhere on earth.

✉ 12–14 Long Acre ☎ 020 7836 1321; www.stanfords.co.uk 🚇 Leicester Square

DEPARTMENT STORES

John Lewis

With helpful staff and a motto of 'Never knowingly undersold', this seven-storey flagship department store is a British favourite: stylish and wide-ranging, from trendy kitchen goods in the basement through cosmetics, fashion and household musts.

✉ 300 Oxford Street ☎ 020 7629 7711 🚇 Oxford Circus, Bond Street

Liberty

Famously associated with the art nouveau and developing design oriented printed fabrics, the interior of London's most beautiful store comprises series of four-floor galleries around a central well.

✉ 210–220 Regent Street ☎ 020 7734 1234 🚇 Oxford Circus

Marks & Spencer

This is the biggest branch and the flagship of one of Britain's favourite stores with high quality and value across its range.

✉ 458 Oxford Street ☎ 020 7935 7954 🚇 Marble Arch

Selfridges

The magnificent art deco and Ionic pillar frontage promises more than the store actually delivers. Probably best for clothes, though there's also a good food hall and a huge perfume department.

✉ 400 Oxford Street ☎ 0800 123 400 🚇 Bond Street

FASHION
Topshop

Super model Kate Moss designs just one of the ranges in this flagship store; three floors offer trendy, affordable fashion for younger women and teenagers.

✉ 36–38 Great Castle Street ☎ 020 7636 8040 🚇 Oxford Circus

FOOD AND DRINK
Neal's Yard Dairy

Splendid rustic-style shop selling mainly British and Irish cheeses. Some French, Italian and Greek cheeses are also available.

✉ 17 Short's Gardens ☎ 020 7240 5700 🚇 Covent Garden

MARKET
Covent Garden Piazza

There are two areas, the Jubilee and Apple markets. The general market is open from Tuesday to Friday, selling everything from clothing to household goods. Mondays are dedicated to antiques dealers. At the weekend, the speciality is arts and crafts.

✉ Covent Garden Piazza 🕐 Mon–Fri 9:30–6; Sat, Sun 9–6 🚇 Covent Garden

ENTERTAINMENT

MUSIC

Jazz 'n' Pizza

London has two very high-quality nightly jazz and pizza restaurants; the Jazz Club Soho and the more classy Pizza on the Park.

✉ Jazz Club Soho, 10 Dean Street ☎ 020 7437 9595 🚇 Tottenham Court Road ✉ Pizza on the Park, 11 Knightsbridge ☎ 020 7235 7825 🚇 Hyde Park Corner

Roadhouse

A 1950s US-themed live-music bar and diner with a mainly 30-something crowd getting down to blues, funk and classic rock.

✉ Jubilee Hall, 35 The Piazza ☎ 020 7240 6001 🚇 Covent Garden

Ronnie Scott's

The place to see the best jazz in the capital. There are generally two sets per night, one at 8:30pm and the other at 11pm.

✉ 47 Frith Street ☎ 020 7439 0747. Booking is advised 🚇 Leicester Square

Royal Opera House

There has been a theatre on this site since 1732 but the theatre is now home to the Royal Ballet and the Royal Opera companies.

✉ Covent Garden ☎ 020 7304 4000; www.roh.org.uk 🚇 Covent Garden

NIGHTLIFE

Madame Jojo's

Madame Jojo's presents everything from rhythm and blues to deep funk to 'tran-tastic' parties.

✉ 8–10 Brewer Street, Soho ☎ 020 7734 3040; www.madamejojos.com 🚇 Piccadilly Circus

THEATRE

Regent's Park Open Air Theatre

This beautiful space has long been London's favourite alfresco venue, staging plays (mostly by Shakespeare) and musicals.

✉ Inner Circle, Regent's Park ☎ 0844 826 4242; www.openairtheatre.org 🕓 Late May–Sep 🚇 Baker Street

Outer London

London is often described as a collection of villages. Over 2,000 years, these communities were slowly amalgamated to make today's sprawling city. However, many original villages still exist, with a special character that makes them well worth a day trip.

The easiest and most popular excursion is downriver to Greenwich, full of history, good shopping and restaurants. Upriver lie Hampton Court Palace and the Royal Botanic Gardens at Kew. Each makes a glorious sunny summer's day out, but don't try to combine the two – there is far too much to see. Return visitors to London should seek out the low-key but highly enjoyable pleasures of riverside Richmond, and Twickenham, on the opposite side of the Thames.

GREENWICH

Greenwich is some 10km (6 miles) east of the centre of London, accessed by train from London Bridge or on the Dockland Light Railway (DLR) direct. Or take a boat to arrive the traditional way, or perhaps the DLR to Island Gardens, directly opposite Greenwich. From here you can enjoy a river view that has changed little in centuries, then simply walk under the Thames via the Greenwich Foot Tunnel. Thanks to its observatory, Greenwich is where the measurement of time was standardised. Greenwich Mean Time, the Meridian Line and Longitude 0° are synonymous with this UNESCO World Heritage Site. Though suffering from heavy traffic and summer crowds, Greenwich retains something of a village atmosphere with lots of interesting shops, a market, an abundance of historic attractions and one of London's finest parks.
www.greenwichwhs.org.uk

🛈 Discover Greenwich ☎ 0870 608 2000 🕐 Daily 10–5 ❓ Guided walking tours depart daily 12:15, 2:15 ☎ 020 8858 6169 🚉 DLR to Cutty Sark

National Maritime Museum

With displays ranging from pirates and slavery to warfare and ecology, every aspect of man and the sea is examined in this world-class maritime museum. Learn about intrepid explorers, take the helm of a Viking ship and get the facts about the Titanic disaster. At its heart is the Neptune Court, a dramatic glassed-over courtyard with the museum's largest objects, such as the carved and gilded state barge made for Frederick, Prince of Wales, in 1732. Near here are 15 or so galleries that explain the history and role of maritime Greenwich, Britain as a once-great sea power and ocean exploration. Some of the finest ship models and great maritime paintings are also here. Younger visitors should head for All Hands and The Bridge, two hands-on galleries.

✉ Greenwich Park ☎ 020 8312 6565 (recorded info); 020 8858 4422 🕐 Daily 10–5. Closed 24–26 Dec 🎟 Free 🍴 The Galley Café (£) 🚉 DLR to Cutty Sark 🚆 Greenwich from London Bridge ⛴ Greenwich Pier

Royal Observatory

The Royal Observatory was founded in 1675 by Charles II to find out the 'so-much desired longitude of places for perfecting the art

of (sea) navigation'. High on a mound in Greenwich Park, and commanding a splendid view, it was designed by Sir Christopher Wren and functioned as Britain's principal observatory until 1957. Today it is a museum that tells the history of the observatory and offers a crash course in the measurement of time and astronomy. Displays are well explained and there is also a fascinating camera obscura. The prime attraction for most visitors, however, is to be photographed standing astride the 0° longitude line (which passes right through the observatory) with one foot in the eastern hemisphere and one foot in the western.

www.nmm.ac.uk

✉ Greenwich Park ☎ See National Maritime Museum opposite 🕐 Daily 10–5. Closed 24–26 Dec 💷 Free 🍴 The Galley Café (£), National Maritime Museum (➤ opposite) Ⓓ DLR to Cutty Sark 🚉 Greenwich from London Bridge 🚤 River boat to Greenwich Pier

Queen's House

This exquisite miniature palace is set at the heart of Greenwich's historic riverfront complex and was the very first classical-style building in England, begun in 1616. It was designed by Inigo Jones. The queen in question was originally Anne of Denmark, wife of James I, though by the time of completion in 1635 she had died and Henrietta Maria, wife of Charles I, assumed tenancy.

✉ Greenwich Park ☎ See National Maritime Museum opposite 🕐 Daily 10–5. Closed 24–26 Dec 💷 Free 🍴 The Galley Café (£), National Maritime Museum (➤ opposite) Ⓓ DLR to Cutty Sark 🚉 Greenwich from London Bridge 🚤 Greenwich Pier

a walk around Greenwich

Greenwich is all about maritime heritage. At the top of the hill, the Royal Observatory provided accurate measurement of time, helping ships improve navigation. You'll also see the *Cutty Sark*, a record-breaking tea clipper (currently undergoing a massive overhaul after a fire).

From the pier, walk up Greenwich Church Street. Turn left in to the historic covered market.

Its boutiques, food, antiques and crafts stalls are liveliest from Wednesday to Sunday.

Exit the market via the top right-hand corner, to King William Walk. Turn right and walk up to Greenwich Park and then follow The Avenue for the brisk climb up the hill that takes you to the Royal Observatory (▶ 159).

The views to Canary Wharf and the O$_2$ Arena are outstanding.

*Walk back down the hill along the path 20m (22yds) to the east of General Wolfe's statue. Exit through the park gate into Park Row. After a few steps, turn left into the grounds of Queen's House (➤ 159) and the National Maritime Museum (➤ 158). Leave the museum, cross Romney Road and enter the **Old Royal Naval College and Chapel**.*

The College is now part of the University of Greenwich and Trinity College of Music. Visit the Chapel (1752) and the grandiose Painted Hall (1703), with its decorated ceiling.

Return to the DLR station.

Distance Approximately 3km (2 miles)
Time 2–4 hours, depending on visits
Start point Greenwich Pier 🚇 DLR to Island Gardens, then pedestrian tunnel 🚇 Greenwich from London Bridge 🚢 River boat to Greenwich Pier
End point Old Royal Naval College
Lunch Picnic in the park

Cutty Sark ☎ 020 8858 3445; www.cuttysark.org.uk ⊗ Closed for refurbishment until 2011

Old Royal Naval College and Chapel
☎ 020 8269 4747; www.oldroyalnavalcollege.org ⊗ Daily 10–5 ⊞ Free

HAMPSTEAD

Leafy Hampstead, London's most famous 'village', was developed as a spa in the 18th century and became a fashionable and exclusive retreat favoured by many prominent writers and artists. Spotting name plaques among the many beautiful former homes of luminaries such as Sir Arthur Bliss, John Keats, Henry Moore, D H Lawrence, John Constable and the like is a favourite visitor pastime. The steep narrow streets around the centre are very well preserved and retain an intimate feel. The most appealing include Flask Walk, Well Walk (where you'll find the original spa fountain), Holly Walk, Hampstead Grove and Church Row. Meanwhile, Hampstead High Street and Heath Street bristle with trendy restaurants, cafés and a good variety of small independent shops that cater to the well-heeled residents.

There are a number of low-key sights in the centre. **Burgh House** (1704) acts as a local museum; **Fenton House** (built in 1693) holds ceramics and a renowned collection of historic keyboard instruments; **Keats House,** where the poet John Keats lived for almost two years, is a delightful spot, where *Ode to a Nightingale* and many other fine poems were written. Just south of here is the **Freud Museum,** where Sigmund Freud lived from 1938 until his death in 1939.

Hampstead's other claim to fame is Hampstead Heath, London's largest and most famous heathland, covering some 320ha (791 acres). The heath is one of north London's favourite summer walking spots and its ponds are also used for swimming. Parliament Hill is a traditional Sunday venue for kite-flying and offers great views across to central London. Much of the heath consists of undeveloped woodland, the main exception being the landscaped grounds of Kenwood House (▶ 166–167).

🚇 Hampstead

Burgh House

✉ New End Square ☎ 020 7431 0144; www.burghhouse.org.uk
🕐 Wed–Sun 12–5 💷 Free

Fenton House

✉ Hampstead Grove ☎ 020 7435 3471; www.nationaltrust.org.uk
🕐 Mar Sat, Sun 11–5; Apr–Oct Wed–Fri 2–5, Sat, Sun 11–5
💷 Moderate

Keats House

✉ Keats Grove ☎ 020 7435 2062 🕐 Easter–Oct Tue–Sun 1–5; Nov–Easter Fri–Sun 1–5 💷 Moderate

Freud Museum

✉ 20 Maresfield Gardens ☎ 020 7435 2002; www.freud.org.uk
🕐 Wed–Sun 12–5 🚇 Finchley Road 💷 Moderate

HAMPTON COURT PALACE

Work on Hampton Court Palace began in 1514 under the tenure of Henry VIII's Lord Chancellor, Cardinal Wolsey. By 1528, however, Wolsey had fallen from favour and Henry had acquired it for himself. He built it up to be the most lavish palace in England where he fêted European royalty and spent five of his six honeymoons. In 1689, William III and Mary II commissioned Sir Christopher Wren to remodel the apartments and to give the palace much of its present-day appearance. George II was the last monarch to use Hampton Court (1760).

For most visitors the surviving Tudor pieces are still the palace highlights: the great gatehouse and a magnificent astronomical clock, the capacious Tudor Kitchens stocked with contemporary foods and utensils, and fires ablaze all year round, the sumptuous centrepiece Great Hall and the Chapel Royal with its breathtaking ornate ceiling.

The King's Apartments (built by William III) are among the finest baroque state apartments in the world and the Wolsey Rooms hold a fine Renaissance picture gallery, though the palace's greatest artwork, *Triumphs of Caesar* by Mantegna, is in the Lower Orangery.

The gardens, planted in the late 17th century, are glorious and include the ever-popular maze, the Great Vine (England's largest) and the Royal Tennis Court. The latter was built in 1626 and real tennis (a forerunner of lawn tennis) is still played here regularly.

www.hrp.org.uk

✉ Hampton Court, East Molesey ☎ 0844 482 7777

🕙 Palace and Maze: Apr–Oct daily 10–6; Nov–Mar 10–4:30 (last admission 1 hour before closing). Formal Gardens: summer daily 10–7; winter 10–5:30. Informal Gardens: summer daily 7am–8pm; winter 7–6. Home Park: May–Jul daily 7am–9pm; Apr, Aug, Sep 7am–8pm; Mar, Oct 7–6; Nov–Feb 7–5:30

💷 All-inclusive ticket to palace and gardens expensive. Maze only inexpensive. Gardens moderate 🍴 Tiltyard café (£) and restaurant (££)

🚇 Train from Waterloo to Hampton Court. Boat from Richmond, Westminster or Kew (summer only) 🚌 111, 216, 411, 451, 513, R68

HIGHGATE

The charming village of Highgate lies just east of Hampstead Heath and like its famous neighbour, Hampstead (▶ 162–163), was a favourite retreat for the upper classes and literary figures, including Samuel Taylor Coleridge (author of *The Rime of the Ancient Mariner*).

Its most popular visitor highlight is Highgate Cemetery. Opened in 1839, the cemetery soon became the fashionable final resting place of politicians, poets, actors and other Victorian personalities. Monuments grew ever larger and more ornate and the cemetery turned into a tourist attraction. The West Cemetery is the real draw, piled high with crumbling catacombs, Egyptian columns and obelisks, ivy-clad vaults and grand mausoleums. It looks like the set for a horror movie and is said to have inspired Bram Stoker (the author of *Dracula*). However, the most famous personalities are buried in the East Cemetery and include Karl Marx, Sir Ralph Richardson, Mary Ann Evans (pen-name George Eliot) and comedian Max Wall.

www.highgate-cemetery.org

✉ Swain's Lane ☎ 020 8340 1834 🕔 East Cemetery Mon–Fri 10–5 (4:30 winter), Sat, Sun 11–4 (3:30 winter). West Cemetery, admission by tour only; Sat–Sun 11–4 each hour, Mon–Fri tours at 2 (advisable to book). Nov–Mar tours at weekends only 11–3 ✋ East Cemetery inexpensive; West Cemetery moderate for tours 🚇 Archway ❓ No children under 8 in the West Cemetery

KENWOOD HOUSE

If you would like to see a real country house without straying too far then visit Kenwood, on the north of

Hampstead Heath (➤ 162–163). Built in 1616, it was remodelled in 1764 by Robert Adam, whose signature pale blue, neoclassical design is apparent as soon as you enter the house. The paintings at Kenwood are known as the Iveagh Bequest and form one of the most important collections bequeathed to the nation. They are mostly 17th- and 18th-century works from the English, Dutch and French schools, though recent additions include much earlier paintings by Botticelli and Hans Memling. The most famous is a Rembrandt self-portrait, acknowledged as one of his very best. Also notable are works by Frans Hals and Vermeer. New acquisitions include Constable's *Hampstead Heath with Pond and Bathers*. The architectural *tour de force* of the house is the library, with its elaborately decorated tunnel-vaulted ceiling and Corinthian columns. It is considered one of Adam's finest interiors.

The gardens have featured in films such as *Notting Hill*. On summer evenings, the grassy amphitheatre is transformed in to one of London's most popular outdoor music venues for the Kenwood House Picnic Concerts (picnics are sold on site), attracting jazz, rock and classical music stars.
www.english-heritage.org.uk

✉ Hampstead Lane ☎ 020 8348 1286 🕐 House daily 11:30–4; park stays open longer. Closed 24–25 Dec, 1 Jan 💷 Free (charge: exhibitions)
🍴 Restaurant, café (£–££) 🚇 Archway

KEW, ROYAL BOTANIC GARDENS

Founded in the mid-18th century, Kew Gardens, a huge park of almost 122ha (300 acres), holds a marvellous collection of plants, trees and flowers from every corner of the globe. Most of the species are grown outdoors, but huge glass and wrought-iron greenhouses replicate exotic climes. The most spectacular of these is the curvy Palm House, built between 1844 and 1848. The Temperate House was the world's largest greenhouse when built in 1899 and contains a Chilean Wine Palm some 16m (52ft) tall and over 150 years old. The Princess of Wales Conservatory is a favourite for its giant water-lily pads, and the exhibition Evolution is a high-tech exploration of the story of the planet to date.

Reminders of the gardens' early royal patronage are provided by tiny Kew Palace (summer home of George III 1802–18), Queen Charlotte's Cottage and the Queen's Garden. The gardens are a

UNESCO World Heritage Site, and, in 2009, celebrated their 250th birthday.

www.kew.org

✉ Kew, Richmond ☎ 020 8332 5655 🕐 Daily from 9:30. Closes approx 4:15 winter, 6:30 summer. Closed 25 Dec, 1 Jan 💷 Expensive 🍴 Café (£), restaurants (£–££) 🚇 Kew Gardens 🚢 Riverboat to Kew Pier from Westminster and Richmond (Apr–Oct) ❓ Kew Explorer hop-on hop-off land train (moderate). The Xstrata Treetop walkway 18m (59ft) above the ground gives a unique view of the canopy

RICHMOND AND TWICKENHAM

These adjoining riverside suburbs make up one of London's most charming and bucolic districts. From Richmond station turn left to walk along George Street. Off here to the right is a lovely village green. Return to George Street and continue to Richmond Bridge and the impressive classical-style riverside development. To visit Richmond Park take bus 371 and get off at the Royal Star & Garter; here you can enjoy the magnificent view down on to the river.

Richmond Park, London's largest royal park and one of its wildest, with herds of deer, is ideal for a picnic. If you want to explore it properly consider renting a bicycle. As an alternative to the park, follow the towpath along the river from Richmond Bridge (it's possible to cycle along here) and after around 30 minutes you will reach **Ham House.** This is an outstanding 17th-century house that has been refurbished to its former glory.

Nearby is the 82,000-seat **Twickenham Stadium,** the headquarters of both the England and international game. Matches are played between August and May, but year-round you can take a Twickenham Stadium Tour to see the players' dressing rooms and players' tunnel. For a history of the sport, visit the World Rugby Museum, with its interactive displays that help to recreate the sound, sights and smell of the sport.

Ham House

✉ Ham Street, Ham ☎ 020 8940 1950;
www.nationaltrust.org.uk ⏰ House: Apr–Oct
Sat–Wed 12–4. Gardens: all year Sat–Wed 11–6
✋ Moderate

Twickenham Stadium

✉ Rugby Road ☎ 0208 892 8877 ⏰ Tue–Sun 10–5; closed match days
✋ Expensive 🚉 London Waterloo to Twickenham, then 15 min walk

V&A MUSEUM OF CHILDHOOD

The Museum of Childhood started life in 1856 in South Kensington as a temporary wing of the Victoria and Albert Museum. Its elaborate, typically Victorian ironwork structure was then moved wholesale to Bethnal Green. Imaginative refurbishment has kept the spirit of the past, while adding a new, dynamic approach, ensuring that education is fun. It is still part of the V&A and is a shrine to childhood and all the accoutrements that go with it, from birthing stools to children's wartime gas masks, from Javanese shadow puppets and Steiff teddy bears to Sonic the Hedgehog and Teletubbies.

The museum is as much for adults as for children, documenting social trends and changes through the medium of play. Many toys date back centuries and several are exquisite hand-made pieces. The museum is particularly renowned for its collection of doll's houses: the Nuremberg House dates back to 1673. Its doll collection is also comprehensive and includes some outstanding Japanese ceremonial dolls. There are activities suitable for both children and adults, including games, arts and crafts tables, themed paper trails, special events, workshops, and movie and theatre productions.

www.vam.ac.uk

✉ Cambridge Heath Road, Bethnal Green ☎ 020 8983 5200 ⏰ Daily
10–5:45 ✋ Free; small charge for some activities 🍴 Benugo Café (£)
🚇 Bethnal Green ❓ Lovely park for picnics

HOTEL

Number 16 (£)

In a Victorian terrace house (row house), this small bed-and-breakfast is run by actor and TV personality Robert Gray.

✉ St Alfege Passage, Greenwich ☎ 020 8853 4337; www.st-alfeges.co.uk
🚇 Greenwich DLR

The Kings Arms Hotel (££)

Next to Hampton Court's Lion Gate, this 350-year-old coaching inn offers comfy rooms and traditional food. Some four-poster beds.

✉ Hampton Court Road, Hampton Court ☎ 020 8977 1729;
www.hamptoncourthotel.com 🚇 Hampton Court

Inn at Kew Gardens (££)

Part hotel, part gastropub, this Victorian coaching inn provides a relaxing alternative to staying in London itself.

✉ 292 Sandycombe Road, Kew ☎ 020 8940 2220;
www.capitalpubcompany.com 🚇 Kew Gardens

RESTAURANTS

Flask Tavern (£)

Legend has it that highwaymen hid here. From the Sunday roast beef lunches to the 200-year-old wood panelling, this is a classic British pub.

✉ 77 Highgate West Hill, Highgate ☎ 020 8348 7346 🕐 Daily 12–11
🚇 Archway, Highgate

Ma Cuisine (£–££)

Set in a former post office, this Kew bistro serves French classics: cassoulet and coq au vin, lemon tart and French cheeses.

✉ 9 Station Approach, Kew ☎ 020 8332 1923 🕐 Daily 10–11:30
🚇 Kew Gardens

Cricketers (£)

A popular pub overlooking a green (but urban) cricket field. Hearty food, draft beer.

✉ The Green, Richmond ☎ 020 8940 4372 🕐 Daily 12–11 🚇 Richmond

Excursions

Bath   174–175

Cambridge   176–177

Oxford   177

A walk around Oxford   178–179

Windsor   180

BATH

Designated as a UNESCO World Heritage Site, the honey-coloured city of Bath was developed as a fashionable spa in the 18th century and is a perfect example of a Georgian town. It was the **Roman Baths** that first established the city and, still remarkably complete, they form the most impressive Roman remains in Britain. Adjacent is another must-see site, Bath Abbey, dating mostly from the 16th century. A short walk away is the Royal Crescent, built between 1767 and 1774. This glorious terrace of 30 classically inspired three-floor houses in glowing golden Bath stone is often claimed to be the most majestic street in Britain.

Just outside Bath, at Claverton, is the excellent **American Museum**, which features 15 authentically re-created 17th- to 19th-century rooms.

www.visitbath.co.uk

🅸 Abbey Church Yard ☎ 0844 847 5257 🕓 Mon–Sat 9:30–6 (5 in winter), Sun 10–4

Roman Baths

✉ Abbey Church Yard ☎ 01225 477785; www.romanbaths.co.uk 🕓 Jan–Feb, Nov–Dec daily 9:30–5:30; Mar–Jun, Sep–Oct 9–6; Jul–Aug 9am–10pm (last admission 1 hour before closing) 💷 Expensive

American Museum

✉ Claverton Manor, Bath ☎ 01225 460503; www.americanmuseum.org 🕓 Mid-Mar to Oct Tue–Sun 12–5 💷 Moderate

CAMBRIDGE

Cambridge is famous for its university, one of the oldest and most prestigious in Britain, alongside Oxford. The oldest college is Peterhouse, founded in 1284, but the most noted college is King's, established in 1441 and renowned for its magnificent medieval architecture and almost heavenly choir. Outstanding among the other 31 colleges are Queen's, Trinity, St John's, Magdalene, Clare, Jesus and Emmanuel. To learn more, take one of the regular walking tours from the Visitor Information Centre.

The Backs is a strip of grassy meadow-cum-lawns between the rear of the colleges and the River Cam. It is a fine venue for a picnic and is a good place for college-viewing. Spanning the Cam are two famous bridges: the Bridge of Sighs, a copy of the famous Venetian bridge; and the Mathematical Bridge, a wooden crossing now bolted together but originally assembled without a single metal fixing. The town's principal museum is the **Fitzwilliam Museum**, with

outstanding collections of paintings, antiquities, ceramics and armour.

🛈 Wheeler Street ☎ 0871 226 8006 (premium rate); www.visitcambridge.org

🕐 Mon–Fri 10–5:30, Sat 10–5 (and Sun 11–3 in summer)

Fitzwilliam Museum

✉ Trumpington Street ☎ 01223 332900; www.fitzmuseum.cam.ac.uk 🕐 Tue–Sat 10–5, Sun 12–5. Closed Mon (except Easter Mon and Spring public hol Mon), Good Fri 🖐 Free ❓ Music Sun 1:15

OXFORD

Oxford is synonymous with its university, the oldest in Britain, with historically interesting colleges, such as Christ Church, New College and Magdalen. Oxford also has plenty of non-university attractions, including the **Ashmolean Museum,** home to one of Britain's finest provincial collections, and the Pitt Rivers Museum, a delightfully old-fashioned Victorian ethnographic treasure-trove. The Covered

Market, selling food and clothing plus all sorts of other things, is also worth a visit.

www.visitoxford.org

🛈 15–16 Broad Street ☎ 01865 252200 🕐 Mon–Sat 9:30–5, Sun, hols 10–4

Ashmolean Museum

✉ Beaumont Street ☎ 01865 278000 🕐 Tue–Sat and public hols 10–5, Sun 12–5 🖐 Free

a walk around Oxford

Start from the tourist information centre, where you can pick up maps and leaflets.

On the left is Christ Church College, one of the university's largest.

Continue to the wrought iron gates; turn left and walk through the War Memorial Garden. Turn left on the path between the stone wall and the playing field; go through the gate.

On your left is Corpus Christi College; on the right, Merton.

Cross Merton Street; follow Magpie Lane to High Street.

Opposite is the University Church of St Mary the Virgin. A walkway on the left side leads to Radcliffe Square, dominated by the Radcliffe Camera, Britain's first circular library, opened in 1749.

Exit the square on the left, on Brasenose Lane. Turn right on Turl Street, lined with colleges and right again onto Broad Street.

Here, Oxford fixtures include Blackwell, a renowned bookshop and the 17th-century **Sheldonian Theatre**. Climb to the cupola for a view of Oxford's 'dreaming

spires'. Next is the **Bodleian Library**. Join a tour to see the magnificent Duke Humfrey's Library and Divinity School, a masterpiece of Gothic architecture.

Turn right onto Catte Street and left onto New College Lane, beneath Oxford's very own Bridge of Sighs.

For a pub lunch, turn immediately left into St Helen's Passage and follow it to the Turf Tavern.

Return to New College Lane, turn left and continue past New College and St Edmund Hall. At High Street, turn left and walk to Magdalen College, pronounced 'Mordlin'.

This college is worth visiting for its gardens and the sung evening service at 6pm, most days.

Distance Approx 5km (3 miles)
Time 4–6 hours depending on which colleges are open
Start point Tourist information centre ✉ 15 Broad Street
End point Magdalen College
Lunch Turf Tavern (£) ✉ 4 Bath Place, via St Helen's Passage

Sheldonian Theatre ✉ Broad Street ☎ 01865 277299
🕐 Mon–Sat 10–12:30, 2–4:30 (3:30 in winter). All times subject to functions 🖐 Inexpensive

Bodleian Library ✉ Broad Street ☎ 01865 277224 🕐 Guided tours all year Mon–Sat 10:30, 11:30, 2, 3 🖐 Moderate

❓ To find out which colleges are open visit www.ox.ac.uk and follow the Visitors link

WINDSOR

Windsor is famous above all for its spectacularly sited **castle,** which (like the Tower of London) dates back to the time of William the Conqueror and has been continuously occupied since the 11th century. It has been enlarged and remodelled many times, though it took on its basic present shape in the 12th and 14th centuries. The largest occupied castle in the world is both a private home, where the Queen usually spends weekends, and a Royal residence, for ceremonial duties from State Visits to investitures, such as the Order of the Garter ceremony.

The most impressive of all the castle buildings is St George's Chapel, a masterpiece of English Gothic architecture, completed in 1511. Ten monarchs lie here, including Henry VIII and Charles I. The state apartments are hung with works from the Royal Collection, though the most startling exhibit is Queen Mary's Doll's House. Made in 1921 for the consort to King George V, it was designed in meticulous detail at one-twelfth life-size with working plumbing and elevators, and miniature paintings and books donated by eminent writers and artists of the day.

Windsor town is a busy shopping centre but you can escape the crowds by exploring Windsor Park, perfect for a picnic.

www.windsor.gov.uk

🅸 The Old Booking Hall, Windsor Royal Station ☎ 01753 743900

🕐 Mon–Fri, Sat 10–5, Sun 10–4. Extended hours in summer

Windsor Castle

✉ Entrance on Castle Hill ☎ 020 7766 7304; 24-hour recorded information 01753 831118 🕐 Mar–Oct daily 9:45–5:15; Nov–Feb 9:45–4:15. St George's Chapel open Mon–Sat; services only on Sun. Castle/apartments are occasionally closed; reduced admission on these days 🖑 Very expensive

HOTELS

BATH

Bath Tasburgh (£–££)

Set in beautifully tended grounds, this charming Victorian house has views over the Avon Valley. The individually appointed rooms are named after British literary giants. There's a dining room, and a beautiful conservatory where breakfast is served.

✉ Warminster Road ☎ 01225 25096; www.bathtasburgh.co.uk

Bloomfield House (£)

Using organic, Fairtrade and local produce, this sets new standards for B&Bs. Set in a 200-year-old mansion 1 mile (1.5km) from town. Bus stop outside.

✉ 146 Bloomfield Road ☎ 01225 420105; www.ecobloomfield.com

CAMBRIDGE

Arundel House (£–££)

The Arundel looks out onto the river and open parkland. Ask for the bedrooms in the converted coach house, some of which overlook the tranquil Alexander Gardens.

✉ Chesterton Road ☎ 01223 367701; www.arundelhousehotels.co.uk

OXFORD

Burlington House (£)

In a Victorian townhouse, this elegant and comfortable B&B has collected well-deserved awards ever since it opened. Fine breakfasts are served.

✉ 374 Banbury Road ☎ 01865 513513; www.burlington-house.co.uk

WINDSOR

The Christopher (£)

Just across the bridge over the River Thames from Windsor, this 1711 coaching inn is close to Eton College, galleries, antiques shops and restaurants and within a short walk of the castle. Many of the 33 rooms are suitable for families.

✉ 110 High Street, Eton ☎ 01753 852359; www.thechristopher.co.uk

RESTAURANTS

BATH

Moon and Sixpence (£–££)

Set in the old main post office in the very heart of Roman Bath, the Moon and Sixpence serves excellent-value lunches and dinners. There is an upstairs bar, a conservatory and courtyard for summer dining.

✉ 27 Milsom Place ☎ 01225 320088 🕐 Daily 12–2:30, 6–10, later at weekends

No 5 Restaurant (£)

Chef/owners Richard and Carol de Cesare focus on light French and Mediterranean dishes. Jazz on Tuesdays.

✉ 5 Argyle Street ☎ 01225 444 499 🕐 Daily lunch, dinner

The Pump Room (£–££)

Built in 1795, the decadently grand Pump Room was once the social heart of the spa city and is still a popular place. Here you can taste the spa water and take the traditional lunch or tea.

✉ Stall Street (part of the Roman Baths complex) ☎ 01225 444477 🕐 Daily 9:30–5

Sally Lunn's (£)

Savour the atmosphere of Bath's oldest house, built in 1482, while tucking into the famous (brioche-like) Bath Bun. Full meals also served. There's a kitchen museum in the cellar.

✉ 4 North Parade Passage ☎ 01225 461634 🕐 Mon–Sat 10–10, Sun 11–10

CAMBRIDGE

Restaurant 22 (££)

In a Victorian house, Armando and Sharon Tommaso serve classic French and English dishes with a modern twist. If you are luck the 6-hour braised beef may be on the menu.

✉ 22 Chesterton Road ☎ 01223 351880 🕐 Tue–Sat 7–9:45

Cotto (£)

Popular with students and their parents, this café-restaurant buys locally, uses Fairtrade products and offers an international range of dishes.

✉ 183 East Road ☎ 01223 302010 🕐 Tue–Wed 9–3; Thu–Sat 9–3, 7–late

OXFORD
Branca (£)

Chic Italian restaurant serving a wide range of pizzas, risottos and pasta, as well as fish and meat dishes.

✉ 111 Walton Street ☎ 01865 556111 🕐 Daily 12–11

Brown's (£–££)

Buzzing, informal restaurant with a wide range of popular classic brasserie dishes at reasonable prices.

✉ 5–11 Woodstock Road ☎ 01865 511995 🕐 Mon–Sat 11am–11:30pm, Sun noon–11 (last orders 9)

Turf Tavern (£)

Up an ancient alleyway, this pub has a history dating back to the 14th century. Hearty student-oriented pub grub.

✉ 7 Bath Place, off Holywell Street ☎ 01865 243235 🕐 Mon–Sat 11–11, Sun 12–10:30

WINDSOR
Bel and the Dragon (£–££)

In this 11th-century ale house, the rustic tables and chairs contrast with the trendy modern British and Mediterranean-influenced cooking.

✉ Thames Street ☎ 01753 866056 🕐 Mon–Sat, lunch, dinner; Sun 12–9

Gilbey's Bar and Restaurant (£–££)

Reserve a table at this popular restaurant just over the footbridge spanning the Thames, dividing Windsor and Eton. Good inventive menu and very reasonable wine prices.

✉ 82–83 High Street, Eton ☎ 01753 854921 🕐 Daily lunch, dinner

Index

accommodation 88–89, 108, 125, 136–137, 151, 171, 181
activities 60–61
afternoon tea 15, 18, 61
airports and air travel 26, 27
Albert Memorial 133
American Museum, Bath 175
Apsley House 128
Ashmolean Museum, Oxford 177

banks 32
Bank of England Museum 94
Banqueting House 76
Barbican 110
Bath 174–175
Bethnal Green, V&A Museum of Childhood 170
Big Ben 41
Bloomsbury 141
Bodleian Library, Oxford 179
Bond Street 70
Borough Market 61, 112
brass rubbings 86
Brick Lane Market 19, 110
British Museum 36–37
Buckingham Palace 76–78
Burgh House 162, 163
Burlington House 82
buses 16, 27

Cabinet War Rooms and Churchill Museum 79
Cambridge 176–177
Canary Wharf 63
Carnaby Street 70
car rental 29
Cartoon Museum 68, 142
Cenotaph 87
Changing of the Guard 61, 77–78
Chapel of St John 51
Chapel of St Peter ad Vincula 51
Chapel Royal 83
Charles Dickens Museum 94–95
Chelsea 128–129, 130–131
Chelsea Old Church 131
Chelsea Physic Garden 131
children's attractions 68–69
church concerts 19
City of London 93
Clarence House 83
classical music 110, 126, 156
climate 22, 31
Clink Prison Museum 112–113
Clock Museum 97
coaches 26
concessions 29
Courtauld Gallery 95
Covent Garden 70, 144–145, 155

Covent Garden Piazza 38–39, 70
Crown Jewels 51
Croydon 11
Cutty Sark 160, 161

dance 126
dental treatment 23
Design Museum 113
Diana, Princess of Wales 133
Dickens, Charles 66, 94–95
Docklands 62–63, 96
Docklands Light Railway (DLR) 62–63, 96, 158
Downing Street 87
Dr Johnson's House 97
drinking water 32
driving 28–29
drugs and medicines 31–32
Duck Tours 69

eating out 58–59, 89–90, 108–109, 125, 137–139, 151–153, 171, 182–183
electricity 32
Elizabeth II, Queen 80
embassies and consulates 31
emergency telephone numbers 31
entertainment 92, 110, 126, 140, 156
Eros statue 81
events and festivals 24–25
excursions from London 172–183

fares 29
Fenton House 162, 163
ferries 26
Fitzwilliam Museum, Cambridge 176, 177
Fleet Street 96–97
food and drink 12–15, 92, 155
see also eating out
Fountain Court 100
Freud Museum 162, 163

gentlemen's clubs 84
geography 10–11
Golden Hinde 68
government 11
Gray's Inn 98, 101
Greenwich 158–161
Greenwich Park 65, 159
Guildhall 97

Ham House 169, 170
Hamleys 68
Hampstead 162–163
Hampstead Heath 162–163, 166

Hampton Court Palace 164–165
Harrods 129, 139
health 22, 23, 31–32
Highgate 166
Highgate Cemetery 166
HMS Belfast 114
Holmes, Sherlock 148
Horse Guards 87
hotels, see accommodation
Houses of Parliament 40–41
Hyde Park 132

Imperial War Museum 115
Inner temple 98
Inns of Court 19, 98, 100–101
internal flights 27

jazz venues 156
Jermyn Street 79
Jewel Tower 116

Keats House 162, 163
Kensington Gardens 133
Kensington High Street 70
Kensington Palace 133
Kenwood House 163, 166–167
Kew 168–169
King's Road 71
Knightsbridge 71

language 33
Leighton House 134
Lincoln's Inn 98, 101
Little Angel Theatre 68
Lloyd's Building 98
London Brass Rubbing Centre 86
London Coliseum 92
London County Hall 116
London Dungeon 117
London Eye 65, 118–119
London Pass 29
London Transport Museum 142–143

Madame Tussaud's 146
Marble Arch 132
markets 19, 61, 110, 126, 139
Middle Temple 98, 100
money 30
Monument 65, 98
Museum of London 102–103
Museum of London Docklands 96
museum opening times 32
music venues 92, 110, 126, 156

National Army Museum 134–135
National Gallery 42–43
national holidays 24

National Maritime Museum 158
National Portrait Gallery 80
National Theatre 126
Natural History Museum 44–45
Neal's Yard 70, 145, 153
Nelson, Admiral Lord 47, 75, 85, 86
Nelson's Column 75, 86

Old Royal Naval College and Chapel 161
Olympics, Summer 2012 11
opening hours 32
opera 92, 156
Oxford 177, 178–179
Oxford Street 71
Oxo Tower 65, 119

Palace of Westminster 40–41, 116
parks and gardens 17, 65, 131, 132, 164–165, 168–169
Parliament Hill 65, 163
passports and visas 22
personal safety 32
Peter Pan statue 133
Petticoat Lane 110
pharmacies 31, 32
Piccadilly 71
Piccadilly Circus 81
Pitt Rivers Museum, Oxford 177
Poets' Corner 55
police 31, 32
Pollock's Toy Museum 69
population 11
Portobello Road 19, 61
postal services 31, 32
public transport 27
pubs 18, 66–67, 108–109, 151–152

Queen Mary's Doll's House 180
Queen Mary's Rose Garden 147
Queen's Gallery 77, 78
Queen's House 159

Regent Street 71
Regent's Park 146–147
Regent's Park Open-Air Theatre 147, 156
Richmond 169–170
Richmond Park 169
Ripley's Believe It or Not! 81
river transport 27
river trips 17, 65
Roman Baths, Bath 175
Royal Academy of Arts 82

Royal Albert Hall 140
Royal Botanic Gardens see Kew
Royal Hospital Chelsea 130–131
Royal Mews 77, 78
Royal Observatory 159
Royal Opera House 156
Royal Shakespeare Company 110

Saatchi Gallery 135
St Bartholomew the Great 103
St Bride's Church 96, 104
St George's Chapel 180
St James's Church 82–83
St James's Palace 83
St James's Park 84
St James's Street 84–85
St Katharine Docks 62, 63, 104–105
St Martin-in-the-Fields 86
St Paul's Cathedral 46–47, 65
St Paul's Church (Actor's Church) 39, 144
St Stephen Walbrook 105
Science Museum 48–49
SEALIFE London Aquarium 116
senior citizens 29
Serpentine Gallery 132
Shakespeare, William 120
Shakespeare's Globe 120
Sheldonian Theatre, Oxford 178, 179
Sherlock Holmes Museum 148
shopping 32, 70–71, 91–92, 110, 126, 139–140, 153–155
Sir John Soane's Museum 106
Sloane Street 71
Soho 148
Somerset House 95
Southbank Centre 126
Southwark 121
Southwark Cathedral 121
Speakers' Corner 132
Spencer House 85
sport and leisure 60–61
State Apartments, Kensington Palace 133
State Rooms, Buckingham Palace 76–77, 78
students 29
Swiss Re Tower (The Gherkin) 10

Tate Britain 122
Tate Modern 65, 123
taxis 28
telephones 31
Temple Church 100–101
theatre 68, 110, 126, 156
time differences 23
tips and gratuities 30

Tomb of the Unknown Warrior 54
tourist offices 23, 30
Tower Bridge 65, 106–107
Tower Bridge Exhibition 107
Tower of London 50–51
Trafalgar Square 86
traffic congestion 29
trains 26, 27
Traitors' Gate 51
travelling to London 26
Trocadero 81
Twickenham Stadium 169–170

underground (tube) 27

V&A Museum of Childhood, Bethnal Green 170
Victoria and Albert Museum (V&A) 52–53
views of London 64–65

walks
    Chelsea 130–131
    Covent Garden 144–145
    Docklands 62–63
    Greenwich 160–161
    Inns of Court 100–101
    Oxford 178–179
Wallace Collection 149
Waterloo Bridge 19, 65
websites 23
Wellington, Duke of 47, 85, 128, 135
Wellington Museum see Apsley House
Westfield London 71
Westminster Abbey 54–55
Westminster Cathedral 124
Whitehall 87
Windsor 180
Windsor Castle 180
Windsor Park 180
World Rugby Museum 169
Wren, Sir Christopher 46, 47, 82, 93, 98, 104, 105, 159, 164

ZSL London Zoo 150

Street Index

Abingdon Street **12D**
Albany Street **28T**
Albert Embankment **12B**
Aldermanbury **21K**
Aldersgate Street **20L**
Aldgate **23K**
Aldgate High Street **23K**
Aldwych **17K**
Alie Street **24K**
Ambrosden Avenue **10C**
Appold Street **22L**
Arundel Street **17J**
Atterbury Street **11B**
Baker Street **26R**
Bankside **20J**
Basil Street **6D**
Basinghall Street **21K**
Bayley Street **14L**
Baylis Road **18G**
Bayswater Road **25P**
Beauchamp Place **5D**
Bedford Place **15L**
Bedford Square **14L**
Bedford Street **15J**
Beech Street **20L**
Belgrave Place **7D**
Belgrave Road **9C**
Belgrave Square **7D**
Belvedere Road **17G**
Berkeley Square **28N**
Bermondsey Street **22G**
Bernard Street **15M**
Bethnal Green Road **23M**
Bevis Marks **23K**
Birdcage Walk **10E**
Bishopsgate **22K**
Blackfriars Bridge **19J**
Blackfriars Lane **19K**
Blackfriars Road **19H**
Blandford Street **26Q**
Bloomsbury Street **15L**
Bloomsbury Way **16L**
Borough High Street **20G**
Bouverie Street **18K**
Bow Street **16K**
Braham Street **24K**
Bressenden Place **9D**
Brewer Street **14J**
Brick Lane **24M**
Bridge Place **9C**
Bridge Street **12E**
Broad Sanctuary **11D**
Brompton Road **5C**
Brook Street **27P**
Brushfield Street **23L**

Buckingham Gate **9D**
Buckingham Palace Road **8C**
Bunhill Row **21M**
Burlington Gardens **13J**
Byward Street **23J**
Cadogan Gardens **6C**
Cadogan Square **6C**
Cadogan Street **6C**
Cale Street **5B**
Camomile Street **23K**
Cannon Street **20K**
Carey Street **17K**
Carnaby Street **13K**
Carter Lane **19K**
Carthusian Street **19L**
Cavendish Place **28Q**
Cavendish Square **28Q**
Chancery Lane **17K**
Charing Cross Road **15K**
Charterhouse Street **18L**
Cheapside **20K**
Chelsea Bridge Road **7B**
Chelsea Embankment **7A**
Chelsea Manor Street **5A**
Chenies Street **14L**
Chesham Place **7D**
Chiswell Street **21M**
City Road **21M**
Clerkenwell Road **18M**
Cleveland Row **13H**
Clink Street **21H**
Cliveden Place **7C**
Cockspur Street **15H**
Commercial Street **24L**
Conduit Street **13J**
Constitution Hill **8E**
Cornhill **22K**
Cornwall Gardens **2D**
Coventry Street **14J**
Cowcross Street **19L**
Cranbourn Street **15J**
Cranley Gardens **3B**
Cromwell Road **1C**
Crucifix Lane **22G**
Cumberland Gate **25N**
Curtain Road **22M**
Curzon Street **8F**
Davies Street **27P**
Devonshire Street **27R**
Dorset Square **25R**
Draycott Avenue **5C**
Draycott Place **6B**
Drayton Gardens **3B**
Druid Street **23G**
Drury Lane **16K**

Duke Of Wellington Place **8E**
Duke's Place **23K**
Duke Street Hill **21H**
Earl's Court Gardens **1C**
Eastcheap **22J**
East Smithfield **24J**
Eaton Gate **7C**
Eaton Square **7C**
Ebury Bridge **8B**
Ebury Bridge Road **8B**
Ebury Street **8C**
Eccleston Street **8C**
Edgware Road **25P**
Elizabeth Street **8C**
Elystan Place **5B**
Elystan Street **5B**
Endell Street **15K**
Exhibition Road **4D**
Farringdon Road **18L**
Farringdon Street **19K**
Fenchurch Street **22J**
Fetter Lane **18K**
Finsbury Circus **22L**
Finsbury Pavement **21L**
Finsbury Square **22L**
Fleet Street **18K**
Flood Street **5A**
Fore Street **21L**
Francis Street **10C**
Fulham Road **4B**
George Street **26Q**
Gilston Road **3A**
Giltspur Street **19L**
Gloucester Place **25R**
Gloucester Road **2D**
Golden Lane **20M**
Goodge Street **14L**
Goodman's Yard **24J**
Goswell Road **19M**
Gower Street **14M**
Gracechurch Street **22J**
Grafton Way **13M**
Gray's Inn Road **17M**
Great George Street **11E**
Great Marlborough Street **13K**
Great Portland Street **13L**
Great Queen Street **16K**
Great Russell Street **15L**
Great Smith Street **11D**
Great Tower Street **22J**
Great Windmill Street **14J**
Grenville Street **20M**
Gresham Street **20K**
Greycoat Place **10D**
Grosvenor Crescent **7D**

Grosvenor Gardens **8D**
Grosvenor Place **8D**
Grosvenor Road **9A**
Grosvenor Square **27N**
Grosvenor Street **27N**
Guilford Street **16M**
Hans Crescent **6D**
Hans Place **6D**
Hans Road **6D**
Hatfields **18H**
Hatton Garden **18L**
Haymarket **14J**
High Holborn **17L**
Hobart Place **8D**
Holborn **18L**
Holborn Viaduct **19L**
Horseferry Road **11C**
Horse Guards Road **15H**
Houndsditch **23K**
Hunter Street **16M**
Hyde Park Corner **8E**
Hyde Park Gate **2E**
Inner Circle **26S**
Ixworth Place **5B**
Jamaica Road **24G**
James Street **27P**
Jermyn Street **13H**
John Islip Street **11C**
Kensington Gore **3E**
Kensington Road **2E**
King Charles Street **11E**
King Edward Street **20K**
King's Road **6B**
Kingsway **16K**
King William Street **21K**
Knightsbridge **5E**
Langham Place **28Q**
Lansdowne Terrace **16M**
Leadenhall Street **22K**
Leather Lane **18M**
Leicester Square **15J**
Lexham Gardens **1C**
Lime Street **22K**
Lincoln's Inn Fields **17L**
Little Britain **19L**
Little Russell Street **15L**
Liverpool Street **22L**
Lombard Street **21K**
London Wall **20L**
Long Acre **15J**
Long Lane **19L**
Long Lane **21G**
Lower Belgrave Street **8D**
Lower Grosvenor Place **8D**
Lower Sloane Street **7B**

Lower Thames Street **22J**
Lowndes Square **6D**
Lowndes Street **7D**
Ludgate Hill **19K**
Mansell Street **24K**
Marble Arch **25P**
Marlborough Road **13H**
Marloes Road **1D**
Marsham Street **11C**
Marylebone High Street **27R**
Marylebone Road **25R**
Middlesex Street **23L**
Millbank **11B**
Minories **23K**
Monmouth Street **15K**
Montague Place **15L**
Montague Street **15L**
Monument Street **22J**
Moorgate **21K**
Moor Lane **21L**
Mortimer Street **13L**
Mount Street **27N**
Neal Street **15K**
New Bond Street **13J**
New Bridge Street **19K**
New Cavendish Street **27Q**
New Fetter Lane **18K**
Newgate Street **19K**
New Oxford Street **15K**
Northumberland Avenue **15H**
Oakley Street **5A**
Old Bailey **19K**
Old Bond Street **13J**
Old Broad Street **22K**
Old Brompton Road **1B**
Old Church Street **4B**
Old Compton Street **14J**
Onslow Gardens **3B**
Onslow Square **4C**
Orchard Street **26P**
Osborn Street **24L**
Outer Circle **28T**
Oxford Street **13K**
Paddington Street **26Q**
Page Street **11C**
Palace Gardens Terrace **1F**
Palace Gate **2E**
Pall Mall **14H**
Pall Mall East **14H**
Park Crescent **28R**
Park Lane **26N**
Park Road **25S**
Park Street **26P**
Parliament Square **11E**
Parliament Street **12E**

Pavilion Road **6D**
Pelham Street **4C**
Piccadilly **9F**
Pimlico Road **7B**
Pont Street **6D**
Portland Place **28R**
Portman Square **26P**
Portman Street **26P**
Poultry **21K**
Prescot Street **24J**
Prince Consort Road **3D**
Prince's Street **21K**
Quaker Street **24M**
Queen's Gate **3C**
Queen Street Place **21J**
Queen Victoria Street **19J**
Redcliffe Gardens **2A**
Regency Street **11C**
Regent Street **13J**
Rochester Row **10C**
Rosebery Avenue **18M**
Royal Hospital Road **6A**
Royal Mint Street **24J**
Russell Square **15M**
St Andrew Street **18L**
St Botolph Street **23K**
St Giles High Street **15K**
St James's Square **14H**
St James's Street **13H**
St John Street **19M**
St Martin's Lane **15J**
St Martin's le Grand **20K**
St Paul's Churchyard **19K**
St Thomas Street **22H**
Savoy Place **16J**
Sclater Street **24M**
Seymour Place **25Q**
Seymour Street **25P**
Shaftesbury Avenue **14J**
Shoe Lane **18K**
Shoreditch High Street **23L**
Shorter Street **24J**
Sloane Avenue **5C**
Sloane Square **7C**
Sloane Street **6D**
Southampton Place **16L**
Southampton Row **16L**
South Lambeth Road **12A**
Southwark Bridge Road **20H**
Southwark Street **19H**
Stable Yard Road **13G**
Stamford Street **18H**
Strand **17K**
Sumner Street **20H**
Sun Street **22L**

Surrey Street **17J**
Sydney Place **4B**
Sydney Street **4B**
Symons Street **7C**
Tachbrook Street **10B**
Temple Avenue **18J**
Temple Lane **18K**
Temple Place **17J**
Thayer Street **27Q**
The Boltons **2B**
The Cut **18G**
The Little Boltons **2B**
The Mall **14H**
The Piazza **16J**
Theobald's Road **17L**
Threadneedle Street **22K**
Thurloe Place **4C**
Tooley Street **23G**
Tottenham Court Road **14M**
Tower Bridge Approach **22H**
Tower Bridge Road **23G**
Tower Hill **23J**

Tudor Street **18K**
Turnmill Street **18M**
Upper Belgrave Street **8D**
Upper Brook Street **26N**
Upper Grosvenor Street **26N**
Upper Ground **17H**
Upper St Martin's Lane **15K**
Upper Thames Street **20J**
Vauxhall Bridge Road **9C**
Vere Street **27P**
Vernon Place **16L**
Vicarage Gate **1E**
Victoria Embankment **17J**
Victoria Road **2D**
Victoria Street **9D**
Villiers Street **16J**
Walbrook **21K**
Walton Street **5C**
Wandsworth Road **12A**
Wardour Street **14K**
Warwick Way **9B**
Waterloo Bridge **17J**

Waterloo Road **17H**
Webber Street **18G**
Welbeck Street **27P**
Wellington Street **16J**
West Smithfield **19L**
Westminster Bridge Road **16G**
Weston Street **22G**
Weymouth Street **27Q**
Whitcomb Street **14J**
Whitechapel High Street **23K**
Whitecross Street **20M**
Whitehall **15H**
Wigmore Street **27P**
Wilton Road **9C**
Woburn Place **15M**
Wood Street **20K**
Wormwood Street **22L**
Worship Street **22M**
Wright's Lane **1D**
York Road **17G**
York Street **25Q**

Acknowledgements

The Automobile Association wishes to thank the following photographers for their assistance in the preparation of this book.

Abbreviations for the picture credits are as follows – (t) top; (b) bottom; (l) left; (r) right; (c) centre; (AA) AA World Travel Library

4l London Eye and River Thames, AA/C Sawyer; **4c** Oxford Circus, AA/M Jourdan; **4r** St Paul's Cathedral, AA/R Strange; **5l** Greenwich Park and Royal Observatory, AA/N Setchfield; **5c** Covent Garden, AA/M Jourdan; **5r** Pulteney Bridge, Bath, AA/C Jones; **6/7** London Eye and River Thames, AA/C Sawyer; **8/9** Regent Street, AA/J Tims; **10/11t** Shakespeare's Globe Theatre, AA/R Turpin; **10/11c** The Tower of London, AA/S McBride; **10cr** Gargoyle, Westminster Abbey, AA/N Setchfield; **10bl** St Paul's Cathedral, AA/N Setchfield; **10br** Changing the Guard, Buckingham Palace, AA/M Jourdan; **11cl** Launceston Place W8, AA/R Turpin; **11bl** Trafalgar Square, AA/M Jourdan; **12bl** Borough Market, Southwark, AA/N Setchfield; **12bc** Borough Market, Southwark, AA/N Setchfield; **12/13** Covent Garden, AA/M Jourdan; **13tr** Borough Market, Southwark, AA/M Jourdan; **14t** St Christopher's Place, AA/N Setchfield; **14b** Roundhouse Cafe, Chalk Farm, AA/N Setchfield; **15tr** Borough Market, Southwark, AA/N Setchfield; **15bl** Neal's Yard, Covent Garden, AA/N Setchfield; **15cr** Food detail, AA/N Setchfield; **15br** Focaccia (flat bread), AA/N Setchfield; **16/17t** Houses of Parliament, AA/B Smith; **17b** Diana, Princess of Wales Memorial Fountain, Hyde Park, AA/N Setchfield; **18tl** Kynance Mews SW7, AA/R Turpin; **18cl** The Audley Pub, AA/L Hatts; **18/19** The Ritz Hotel, AA, **19br** Lincoln's Inn, Chancery Lane, AA/B Smith; **20/21** Oxford Circus, AA/M Jourdan; **25** Parade, Buckingham Palace, AA/M Jourdan; **26** Eurostar train, AA/W Voysey; **27** Canary Wharf station, AA/M Jourdan; **28** Taxi, AA/M Jourdan; **29** Regent Street, AA/J Tims; **31** Telephone box, AA/S McBride; **34/35** St Paul's Cathedral, AA/R Strange; **36tl** British Museum, AA/M Jourdan; **36cl** Elgin Marbles, British Museum, AA; **37t** Queen Elizabeth II Great Court, British Museum AA/N Setchfield; **37cl** Nereid Monument, British Museum, AA/M Trelawny; **38bl** Covent Garden, AA/S McBride; **38/39** Covent Garden, AA/M Jourdan; **39tr** Covent Garden, AA/M Jourdan; **40cl** Big Ben, AA/R Victor; **40/41b** Houses of Parliament,

Sight locator index

This index relates to the maps on the covers. We have given map references to the main sights in the book. Some sights may not be plotted on the maps.

Apsley House **8E**
Bank of England Museum **21K**
Banqueting House **15H**
Borough Market **21H**
British Museum **15L**
Buckingham Palace **9E**
Cabinet War Rooms and Churchill Museum **11E**
Cartoon Museum **15L**
Charles Dickens Museum **17M**
Chelsea **4A**
Clink Prison Museum **21H**
Courtauld Gallery **17J**
Covent Garden Piazza **16J**
Design Museum **24G**
Docklands **24H (off map)**
Fleet Street **18K**
Guildhall **21K**
Harrods **6D**
HMS *Belfast* **22H**
Houses of Parliament **12D**
Hyde Park **5F**
Imperial War Museum **19G (off map)**
Inns of Court **18K**
Jermyn Street **14H**
Jewel Tower **12D**
Kensington Gardens **3F**
Kensington Palace **2E**
Leighton House **1D (off map)**
London County Hall **16G**
London Dungeon **22H**
London Eye **16G**
London Transport Museum **16J**
Lloyd's Building **22K**
Madame Tussaud's **26R**
Monument **22J**
Museum of London **20L**
Museum of London Docklands
National Army Museum **6A**
National Gallery **15J**

National Portrait Gallery **15J**
Natural History Museum **3C**
Oxo Tower **18J**
Piccadilly Circus **14J**
Regent's Park **26T**
Royal Academy of Arts **13J**
Royal Albert Hall
Saatchi Gallery
St Bartholomew the Great **19L**
St Bride's Church **19K**
St James's Church **14J**
St James's Palace **10E**
St James's Park **11E**
St James's Street **13H**
St Katharine Docks **24H**
St Paul's Cathedral **20K**
St Stephen Walbrook **21K**
Science Museum **4D**
SEA LIFE London Aquarium **16G**
Shakespeare's Globe **20J**
Sherlock Holmes Museum **26R**
Sir John Soane's Museum **17L**
Soho **14K**
Southwark Cathedral **21H**
Spencer House **13H**
Tate Britain **11B**
Tate Modern **20H**
Tower Bridge **24H**
Tower of London **23J**
Trafalgar Square **15H**
Victoria and Albert Museum **4D**
Wallace Collection **27Q**
Westminster Abbey **11D**
Westminster Cathedral **10C**
Whitehall **15H**
ZSL London Zoo **16G**

Dear Reader

Your comments, opinions and recommendations are very important to us. Please help us to improve our travel guides by taking a few minutes to complete this simple questionnaire.

You do not need a stamp (unless posted outside the UK). If you do not want to cut this page from your guide, then photocopy it or write your answers on a plain sheet of paper.

Send to: **The Editor, AA World Travel Guides, FREEPOST SCE 4598, Basingstoke RG21 4GY.**

Your recommendations...

We always encourage readers' recommendations for restaurants, nightlife or shopping – if your recommendation is used in the next edition of the guide, we will send you a **FREE AA Guide** of your choice from this series. Please state below the establishment name, location and your reasons for recommending it.

_____
_____
_____
_____
_____
_____

Please send me **AA Guide** _____

About this guide...

Which title did you buy?

AA _____

Where did you buy it?_____

When? m m / y y

Why did you choose this guide? _____
_____
_____
_____
_____

Did this guide meet your expectations?

Exceeded ☐   Met all ☐   Met most ☐   Fell below ☐

Were there any aspects of this guide that you particularly liked? _____
_____
_____
_____

continued on next page...

Is there anything we could have done better? _____

_____

_____

_____

About you...

Name (*Mr/Mrs/Ms*) _____

Address _____

_____

_____ Postcode _____

Daytime tel nos _____

Email _____

Please only give us your mobile phone number or email if you wish to hear from us about other products and services from the AA and partners by text or mms, or email.

Which age group are you in?
Under 25 ☐   25–34 ☐   35–44 ☐   45–54 ☐   55–64 ☐   65+ ☐

How many trips do you make a year?
Less than one ☐   One ☐   Two ☐   Three or more ☐

Are you an AA member? Yes ☐   No ☐

About your trip...

When did you book? m m / y y   When did you travel? m m / y y

How long did you stay? _____

Was it for business or leisure? _____

Did you buy any other travel guides for your trip? _____

If yes, which ones? _____

_____

_____

Thank you for taking the time to complete this questionnaire. Please send it to us as soon as possible, and remember, you do not need a stamp (*unless posted outside the UK*).

| AA | Travel Insurance call 0800 072 4168 or visit www.theAA.com |